# CATHOLICS <u>AND</u> EVANGELICALS

## DO THEY SHARE A COMMON FUTURE?

# CATHOLICS AND EVANGELICALS

## DO THEY SHARE A COMMON FUTURE?

EDITED BY
THOMAS P. RAUSCH

FOREWORD BY RICHARD J. MOUW
AFTERWORD BY EDWARD IDRIS CARDINAL CASSIDY

**InterVarsity Press**
Downers Grove, Illinois

*InterVarsity Press, USA*
*P.O. Box 1400, Downers Grove, IL 60515-1426*
*World Wide Web: www.ivpress.com*
*E-mail: mail@ivpress.com*

*Published by InterVarsity Press, Downers Grove, Illinois, with permission from Paulist Press, Mahwah, New Jersey.*

*InterVarsity Press ®, U.S.A., is the book-publishing division of InterVarsity Christian Fellowship/USA ®, a student movement active on campus at hundreds of universities, colleges and schools of nursing in the United States of America, and a member movement of the International Fellowship of Evangelical Students. For information about local and regional activities, write Public Relations Dept., InterVarsity Christian Fellowship/USA, 6400 Schroeder Rd., P.O. Box 7895, Madison, WI 53707-7895.*

*Cover illustration: Roberta Polfus*

*Interior design: Theresa M. Sparacio*

*ISBN 0-8308-1566-X*

*Printed in the United States of America* ∞

**Library of Congress Cataloging-in-Publication Data**

*Rausch, Thomas P.*
    *Catholics and evangelicals: do they share a common future? / edited by Thomas P. Rausch.*
    *p. cm.*
    *ISBN 0-8091-3986-3 (alk. paper)*
        *1. Catholic Church—Relations—Evangelicalism. 2. Evangelicalism—Relations— Catholic Church. I. Title.*
    *BR1641.C37 C38 2000*
    *280'.042—21*                                                    00-55727
                                                                                    CIP

16  15  14  13  12  11  10   9   8   7   6   5   4   3   2   1
12  11  10  09  08  07  06  05  04  03  02  01  00

# Table of Contents

v

# Acknowledgments

I owe a debt of gratitude to a number of people who helped in the preparation of this book. Chapters One and Two appeared earlier as articles in the British ecumenical journal, *One in Christ*. I am grateful to the editor, Sister Paschal, O.S.B., of Turvey Abbey, Bedfordshire, for permission to use these earlier works. Both have been revised from their original versions.

Dr. Richard J. Mouw, President of Fuller Theological Seminary in Pasadena, contributed the Foreword. Dr. Mouw was one of the founding members of the Los Angeles Catholic/Evangelical Committee (1987), the first local Catholic/Evangelical dialogue in the United States. He has been a friend for many years.

I am particularly grateful to Edward Idris Cardinal Cassidy, President of the Pontifical Council for Promoting Christian Unity. The Cardinal has been particularly interested in Catholic/Evangelical relations and took time out of his busy schedule to contribute the Afterword.

Finally, I want to express my deep gratitude to each of the contributors. May the book be a contribution to the unity for which our Lord Jesus prayed (Jn 17:20–21).

*Thomas P. Rausch, S.J.*
January 1, 2000

For
Jerry L. Sandidge
1939–1992
Pastor (Assemblies of God)
Missionary in Belgium (1972–1982)
Ph.D. in Religious Studies (1985),
Catholic University of Leuven
Pentecostal Ecumenist
*In memoriam*

# Foreword

*Richard J. Mouw*

In 1875 the great American evangelist Dwight L. Moody received a letter from a Catholic monk in Wales. "I must send you one word of affectionate greetings in our Precious Redeemer's name," the monk wrote, "to say how rejoiced I am to hear and read of your powerful gifts from 'The Father of Lights,' good and perfect gifts indeed." The monk went on to assure Moody that while his community engaged in "the perpetual adoration of the Holy Sacrament"—a practice that he knew would make the evangelist nervous—he and his fellow monks also preached "Jesus only as perfect, finished, and present salvation to all who are willing to receive Him. And the only work of the evangelist is to give knowledge of salvation to His people."

Moody was pleased to receive this letter; he seemed to have no doubt that the prayers of these monks were offered up by fellow Christians who had a deep commitment to the cause of the Gospel. In a recent biography of Moody, Lyle Dorsett provides several other examples of how Moody refused to conform to the typical evangelical anti-Catholicism of his day. While living in New England, the evangelist even made a personal contribution to the building fund in a local Catholic parish!

Moody's name was highly revered in the evangelical environs in which I was raised, but no one told me any stories about his friendly relations with Roman Catholics. The evangelicalism of my youth was rigidly anti-Catholic. I regularly heard preachers proclaim with considerable self-confidence that the Pope was the Anti-Christ. I also had first-hand experience with evangelicals who believed that Catholicism was uniformly a religion of "pagan darkness," and that the only hope that any Catholics had was that they might get to heaven "in spite of what their church teaches."

All of this was forever changed for many of us in the evangelical world by the Second Vatican Council. Indeed, it could be argued that the obvious signs of post-Vatican II rapprochement between evangelicals and Catholics is one of the most important ecumenical developments of the past half-century. Not that these developments have ever taken a very "official" shape. The "Evangelicals and Catholics Together" documents, for example, received the endorsement of no ecclesial bodies. The new patterns of cooperation between Catholics and evangelicals have been largely local and ad hoc. This is the kind of arrangement, of course, that suits evangelicals nicely. We have not been much attracted to "conciliar" ecumenism or ambitious denominational mergers. The Billy Graham crusade—where Christians of various denominations work together in a specific evangelistic effort—has been a more natural style of task-oriented ecumenism for us. Our new-found friendships with Roman Catholics, then, has taken the form of what Timothy George has labeled "an ecumenism of the trenches," where evangelicals and Roman Catholics have found common cause on a number of issues that are of concern in the public arena, especially right-to-life matters and other causes associated with the recent "culture wars." But these efforts have also inspired many grassroots evangelicals and Catholics to begin praying and studying the Bible together.

It would be irresponsible, however, simply to ignore theological discussion in all of this. Doctrinal concerns are too important to both of our communities. This is why this book of essays is an important gift to both Catholics and evangelical Protestants. The authors have been intensely involved in Catholic-evangelical dialogue, and they take on the "big" topics on which the two communities have significant disagreements: salvation, ecclesiology, authority, the sacraments, evangelism. There are no attempts here at an easy consensus. But there are serious—and I think quite successful—efforts to get past the long-standing pattern of talking past each other. Important issues are engaged with deep respect and an obvious desire to find real commonalities.

In his 1923 book, *Christianity and Liberalism,* one of the classics of American evangelical thought, J. Gresham Machen—who was in the midst of intense debates with the Protestant liberals of his day—observed that a wide "gulf" existed between evangelical and Catholic thought. "But profound as it is," Machen continued, "it seems almost trifling compared to the abyss which stands between us and many ministers of our own Church." Catholics and evangelicals, said Machen, share a common commitment to the authority of Scripture and the affirmations of the classical creeds.

Machen was wise to highlight the differences between gulfs and abysses. In our "post-Christian" era, the abyss that separates historic Christianity and the culture of unbelief is indeed great. By comparison, while the space that separates evangelicals and Catholics may still be a gulf, it is not nearly as wide as it appeared to be in Machen's day. And the theological bridging efforts represented by these essays are clear evidence that the gap continues to narrow.

# Introduction

*Thomas P. Rausch*

Recently I participated in a Saturday morning conference on the subject of Scripture and tradition sponsored by Pasadena's Fuller Theological Seminary's Orange County campus. The speakers included a Fuller professor from the Orthodox tradition, an evangelical Presbyterian, and myself, a Catholic theologian. Expecting a sparse Saturday morning gathering, I was surprised to find more than eighty people in attendance. As the day unfolded, even more surprising were their backgrounds. While all three traditions were well represented, a number were former Catholics who had become Evangelicals. There were also several in that group who were returning to the Catholic Church, and three former Evangelicals who had joined the Orthodox Church. But the talks were not aimed at making converts. While each speaker explored what was unique to his tradition, the tenor of the day was one of mutual encounter and shared concern for the church's evangelical mission.

This meeting in Orange County was not the only evidence of something new in Catholic/Evangelical relations. The second millennium was the millennium of the divided church. As the third millennium dawns, one of the most encouraging signs is a new interest of Catholics and Evangelicals in each other. Demographics indicate that these two constitute the majority of Christians worldwide. The total number of Roman Catholics has recently passed the 1 billion mark. The number of Evangelicals is approximately 364 million, but may be as high as 400 million.

There have been some remarkable developments. The Roman Catholic Church has been meeting on an international level with Pentecostals since 1972 and with Evangelicals since 1977. The fourth phase of International Catholic/Pentecostal dialogue was completed in 1997;[1] Cecil M. Robeck, Jr., the Dialogue's co-chair, reported on the dialogue's progress personally to Pope John Paul II. Robeck is an Assemblies of God theologian from Fuller Seminary and a contributor to this volume.

Nothing has energized Catholic/Evangelical relations more than "Evangelicals and Catholics Together," an unofficial consultation with representatives from both traditions established in 1993 by Charles Colson and Richard John Neuhaus. The consultation has since produced two statements. "The Christian Mission in the Third Millennium"[2] and "The Gift of Salvation."[3]

ECT was a shock to many Evangelicals. A considerable number were not comfortable with this effort to find common ground with Catholics. A number of books followed the establishment of the consultation, most of them written from a perspective more congenial to conservative or fundamentalist Evangelicals and conservative Catholics. In 1994 John Armstrong edited a volume entitled *Roman Catholicism: Evangelical Protestants Analyze What Divides and Unites Us*.[4] While striving to maintain an irenic tone, the book tends to identify Tridentine Catholicism as the normative expression of the tradition, while dismissing twentieth-century developments in contemporary Catholicism, including those of the Second Vatican Council and certain positions of Pope John Paul II, as infected with theological liberalism and post-Enlightenment modernism. Most of the book's contributors are convinced that Catholics believe and teach a different gospel from that preached by Evangelicals. Thus the book is not an effort to find a common ground in the faith through theological reflection on both traditions. Its real purpose seems to be to call for joint witness against a hostile culture, as well as for a new reformation based on the doctrine of justification by faith alone and an inerrantist understanding of Scripture.

That same year saw the appearance of *Roman Catholics and Evangelicals: Agreements and Differences* by Norman Geisler and Ralph MacKenzie.[5] Also irenic in its approach, this is a far more comprehensive book. But it tends to look on more conservative Catholics as typical representatives of the tradition and fails to take into account mainstream Catholic biblical, historical, and theological scholarship as well as the ecumenical literature of the last thirty years. In spite of these deficiencies, the book represents a step beyond the polemics of the past.

Keith A. Fournier's *A House United: Evangelicals and Catholics Together* also appeared in 1994.[6] Fournier identifies himself as an evangelical Roman Catholic Christian; his very personal account of rediscovering the lost Catholic faith of his childhood through his involvement with Evangelical and Pentecostal Protestantism is eloquent testimony of the appeal of Evangelicalism to many contemporary Catholics. A lawyer, Fournier has worked as executive director of the American Center for Law and Justice, founded by Pat Robertson; he is also the founder of Liberty, Life and Family, an alliance of Christian lawyers, apologists, and activists. Both organizations are "dedicated to pro-liberty, pro-life, and pro-family causes."[7]

In 1995 Colson and Neuhaus brought out *Evangelicals and Catholics Together: Towards a Common Mission*, a collection of essays based on their consultation.[8] Its intent was practical, seeking to bring about greater unity between the two traditions in the face of a hostile culture.

Another volume appeared in 1997, edited by James S.
Cutsinger. Entitled *Reclaiming the Great Tradition: Evangelicals,
Catholics and Orthodox in Dialogue*, the book collected the
papers from what was called "an ecumenical conference for traditional Christians" sponsored by Rose Hill College in South Car-
olina and the Fellowship of Saint James.[9] Its purpose was "to test
whether an ecumenical orthodoxy, solidly based on the classic
Christian faith as expressed in the Scriptures and ecumenical
councils, could become the foundation for a unified and transfor-
mative witness to the present age."[10] A number of the papers
seemed more concerned with battling liberal theology and various
advocacy groups in the culture wars, reflecting the conservative
nature of the conference.

But several papers singled out ecclesiology as an important
issue. Harold O. J. Brown observed that contemporary Protestantism "tends to have a defective view of the fundamental significance of the church."[11] J. I. Packer, in outlining several principles
or guidelines for a persuasive contemporary Christian discourse,
called attention to the church as an "international, supracultural
phenomenon," though like Brown, he acknowledged that for
many Protestants, the church has not played a key role in their
thought.[12] In the epilogue, Carl Braaten cites with approval
Tillich's statement at the beginning of his *Systematic Theology*
that "Theology is a function of the church," but he questions
whether Tillich's understanding of church is the one, holy, catholic
and apostolic church of the Nicene-Constantinopolitan creed.[13]

The purpose of this present book is to try to move the conversation between Catholics and Evangelicals forward. It first
explores the history and present state of their relations. Then it
examines two principal theological issues that have divided
them—the doctrine of salvation and the nature of the church.
Finally, it looks at some signs of progress for the future.

In Chapter One, Cecil M. Robeck, Jr., presents an overview
of Evangelicalism as a Christian movement. He then reviews the
history of the relationship between Catholics and Evangelicals,
their different approaches to faith, some recent developments in

Roman Catholicism, particularly the Second Vatican Council, and some tentative steps toward a greater mutual understanding.

Chapter Two, after summarizing some of the stereotypes that Catholics and Evangelicals have of each other, reviews a number of new signs of cooperation in the areas of youth and renewal ministries, evangelization and development, as well as in relations between Evangelicals and Hispanic Catholics.

The next two chapters focus on salvation. In Chapter Three Robert Louis Wilken studies salvation in early Christian thought. He argues that in the writings of the fathers of the church, salvation is a complex term which embraces both justification and sanctification. He shows that the language and images used by the fathers are drawn from the Scriptures, but that the interpretation of individual texts is based, not on the context of a specific book or author, but rather on the whole of the biblical tradition.

In Chapter Four, Gerald Bray explores salvation from an Evangelical point of view. His essay introduces a number of issues important to that perspective. Among them are the "born again" experience; its "assurance of salvation"; Evangelicalism's debt to Luther, and especially to Calvin; predestination; penal substitution—the Reformation's improvement of Anselm's theory of satisfaction; as well as the sometimes conflicted attitude Evangelicals evidence towards ecumenism.

Chapters Five and Six are on the church. In Chapter Five, Avery Dulles contrasts the distinctive ways Catholics and Evangelicals explicate the biblical images of church as well as the differing ecclesiological perspectives that result. Then he uses the historic "attributes" or "marks" of the church to explore the extent of an Evangelical/Catholic convergence in ecclesiology. Finally he considers the sacraments, the Eucharist, and apostolic ministry, vital concerns for Catholics.

In Chapter Six, Timothy George acknowledges that Evangelicalism has not made ecclesiology a high priority. Yet he recognizes that one of the greatest challenges facing Evangelicals today is precisely how to maintain the "centrality of Gospel truth within ostensibly weak structures of ecclesial authority." His essay seeks to sketch the elements of an evangelical ecclesiology, focusing on the universality of the church; the priority of the Gospel; and the church as One, Holy, Catholic, and Apostolic.

The final chapter, part report, part personal testimony, is David Bjork's account of his experience as evangelical pastor in nominally Catholic France. Sent there by the Missionary Church to establish an evangelical church, he has spent the last twenty years working in Catholic parishes to help Catholics deepen their own faith and ecclesial life. While his work has not been appreciated by some more conservative Evangelicals, it has generally been welcomed by Catholics. It is a great sign of hope for the future.

## Notes

1. See "Evangelization, Proselytism and Common Witness," Statement of the International Dialogue between the Roman Catholic Church and Some Pentecostal Churches and Leaders, in the journal of the Pontifical Council for Promoting Christian Unity, *Information Service* 97 (1998), 38–56.

2. *First Things* No. 43 (May 1994), 15–22.

3. *First Things* No. 79 (January 1998), 20–23.

4. John Armstrong (ed.). *Roman Catholicism: Evangelical Protestants Analyze What Divides and Unites Us* (Chicago: Moody, 1994).

5. Norman L. Geisler and Ralph E. MacKenzie (Grand Rapids, Mich.: Baker Books, 1995).

6. Keith A. Fournier, with William D. Watkins. *A House United: Evangelicals and Catholics Together: A Winning Alliance for the 21st Century* (Colorado Springs: NavPress, 1994).

7. Ibid., 13.

8. Charles Colson and Richard John Neuhaus. *Evangelicals and Catholics Together: Towards a Common Mission* (Dallas: Word, 1995).

9. James S. Cutsinger (ed.). *Reclaiming the Great Tradition: Evangelicals, Catholics and Orthodox in Dialogue* (Downers Grove: InterVarsity Press, 1997).

10. Ibid., 8.

11. Harold O. J. Brown, "Proclamation and Preservation: The Necessity and Temptations of Church Traditions," in *Reclaiming the Great Tradition*, 81.

12. J. I. Packer, "One From Orr: Cultural Crisis, Rational Realism and Incarnational Ontology," in *Reclaiming the Great Tradition*, 174–175.

13. Carl E. Braaten, "Epilogue," in *Reclaiming the Great Tradition*, 188–189.

*Chapter 1*

# Evangelicals and Catholics Together

*Cecil M. Robeck, Jr.*

In May 1994 a group of Evangelical and Roman Catholic leaders, convened by the Evangelical Charles Colson and recent Lutheran-turned-Roman Catholic Richard John Neuhaus, released a statement titled *Evangelicals and Catholics Together: The Christian Mission in the Third Millennium.* It was an open statement, a totally *unofficial* statement, a statement which was first published in the journal of Fr. Neuhaus's Institute on Religion and Public Life, *First Things.*[1]

That same month *Christianity Today,* the flagship of Evangelical news and devotional magazines, led off with an editorial titled "Catholics and Evangelicals in the Trenches." It was not so much an image of soldiers in battle against one another as it was an appeal for openness to this new statement as a symbol of an ecumenism born of frustration—an ecumenical act which depended neither upon formal ecumenical leaders nor on their blessings. It was to be perceived as a capturing of ground which the unnamed editor suggested has "for too long...been left to left-leaning Catholics and mainline Protestants."[2]

So began another discussion in a series of discussions about what, if any, relationship Evangelicals and Roman Catholics might share. I say "another discussion in a series of discussions" because Roman Catholics and Evangelicals have been talking and working together for several decades already, as we shall see later, and Evangelicals and Catholics Together is but the latest salvo to be lobbed into the overall field of discussion. Many of the discussions which are taking place between Evangelicals and Catholics have been taking place at levels which include church leaders and theologians rather than people at the grassroots of the local congregation or parish. And many of the places in which Evangelicals and Roman Catholics have already been working together, even if they are not always willing to acknowledge their cooperation publicly, are in the places where public policy and morality meet.[3]

But if there have been several decades of discussion between Evangelicals and Roman Catholics which suggest greater cooperation than in previous years, there are many areas in which Evangelicals and Roman Catholics are very much at odds with one another. Many of the reasons for this mutual distrust and antagonism lie in a number of the unresolved issues which distinguish Evangelicals from Roman Catholics, issues such as have been outlined in Pope John Paul II's 1995 encyclical on ecumenism, *Ut Unum Sint:* (1) the relationship between Scripture and Tradition, (2) the nature of the Eucharist, (3) the meaning of Ordination to the threefold ministry, (4) the role of the Magisterium, and (5) the role of Mary in the life of the faithful.[4]

Many of the issues which seem to separate Evangelicals from Roman Catholics are felt most profoundly, not at this highly technical theological level—though they are genuinely felt here—but rather they are felt at the pastoral level. They are felt most profoundly when one member of an Evangelical family converts to Roman Catholicism or when a member of a faithful Roman Catholic family converts to some form of Evangelicalism. We may argue together as allies for religious freedom, but when it comes so close to home, we are not so sure that it is a good thing. Interfaith marriages lead to some of the most difficult pastoral and theological problems that the faithful will face in any situation.

Conversion from one denomination to another often leads to deeply held and strongly expressed judgments against the one which was left. I cannot tell you the number of times I have heard Evangelicals testify how thankful they are that they are no longer subject to the meaningless ritual and spiritual darkness that they felt when they were part of the Roman Catholic Church.[5] With such testimonies as background, it is not surprising to hear some Evangelicals simply assume and announce that Roman Catholics are not Christians. This is what one Assemblies of God missionary did when he announced recently that 55 million of the 58 million inhabitants of Italy, most of whom are Roman Catholic, had never even heard the Gospel![6]

Just so that you do not think that this is an issue only for Evangelicals, I note from a recent issue of *Sursum Corda,* a magazine of the so-called "Catholic Renewal," that there is a great deal of triumphalism associated with an article that announced the defection of nearly 150 alumni of Gordon-Conwell Theological Seminary from various Evangelical churches to membership in the Roman Catholic Church.[7] It should come as no surprise, then, that even in the most recent anthology of texts edited by the Vatican Working Group on New Religious Movements, it is stated that "The Christian sects are the most numerous: the majority are Pentecostals; there are Baptists, Adventists and independent denominations. Almost all these groups call themselves 'evangelical churches.'"[8]

But who are these Evangelicals? Where do they come from? What do they really believe? How are they related to those of us who are Roman Catholics? It is to some of these questions that I would like now to turn.

## ◆◆     EVANGELICAL CHRISTIANITY     ◆◆

It is not often easy to define religious movements even when they are Christian. Just think of the diversity which can be found among Roman Catholics themselves. There are many orders, both male and female: Jesuits, Benedictines, Dominicans, Capuchins, Cistercians, Paulists, Franciscans, Sisters of Mercy, Sisters of Charity, Trappists, to name but a few. There are monks and nuns, cloistered and uncloistered, as well as secular clergy. There are congregations which form along racial lines, ethnic lines, linguistic lines, and lines of ritual—the Eastern Rite Catholics, for example. There are Catholics who are fundamentalists. There are Catholics who can be described as liberals. And there are many Catholics in the middle. In spite of all their diversity, they share many things. They do not share everything in the same way, nor do they share everything. Some maintain a deep Marian devotion, while others do not. Some are active participants in the Charismatic Renewal, while others are not. Many of these same generalizations can be made with respect to Protestants.

If we look at Protestantism as a Christian Movement, we see a range of expressions from fundamentalist to liberal. We see those who align with Pentecostalism or with the Charismatic Renewal and those who do not. We see churches and we see parachurch organizations such as Campus Crusade for Christ or Prison Fellowship. On the ecumenical side, we see such organizations as the National Council of the Churches of Christ in the USA as well as the National Association of Evangelicals. Congregations form along racial lines, ethnic lines, and linguistic lines. They share a common past and perhaps a common set of beliefs, but they do not share all things equally.

Evangelicals are part of a Christian movement which is difficult to define. Someone has said that "An Evangelical is a nice Fundamentalist"—a Fundamentalist with a heart, or with a soul. I don't pretend to know whether this is true. What I do know is that the theological landscape of Evangelicalism is multifaceted. It includes great variety in its expression. George M. Marsden, himself an Evangelical and Frances A. McAneney

Professor of History at the University of Notre Dame, has written two very important books which help to define the Evangelical landscape. The first is *Fundamentalism and American Culture: The Shaping of Twentieth-Century Evangelicalism 1870–1925.*[9] In this volume, Professor Marsden helps us to understand first the emergence of Fundamentalism in the United States by beginning with the revivals which came and went along various of the American frontiers. His view is of a Fundamentalism and then an Evangelicalism which is deeply in debt to certain doctrines, battles, and individuals who played key roles in the Reformed wing of Protestantism. In the battles over culture, over the authority of Scripture, over the significance of the Second Coming of Christ for Christian living and for evangelization, it was the conservative wing of Protestantism, particularly of the Reformed ilk—that is, with Swiss, Dutch, and Scottish ancestry and a Presbyterian feel—that developed into American Fundamentalism.

In his second volume, *Reforming Fundamentalism: Fuller Seminary and the New Evangelicalism,* Professor Marsden uses Fuller Seminary, at which I teach, as a foil for describing how certain parts of Fundamentalism in the United States developed into the so-called "New Evangelicalism" of our day.[10] Marsden continues to show the Reformed rootage of the "New Evangelicalism" and he shows how it differs from Fundamentalism. But there are other ways to slice the pie. Donald W. Dayton, Professor of Theology at Northern Baptist Theological Seminary, suggests that Marsden shows a bias here toward the Reformed side of the Church and away from the Methodist side of things.[11] He has suggested in a series of articles that Evangelicalism needs to recognize a Methodist-cum-Holiness-cum-Pentecostal paradigm.[12]

What all of this suggests is that there is great variety to this thing which is called Evangelicalism. It may be that if we were totally fair, we would have to describe a series of *Evangelicalisms* rather than a single Evangelicalism. And you will recognize it in a bewildering variety of manifestations. Perhaps Father Thomas Stransky says it best when he notes:

They come from within the mainline churches (Episcopalian, Presbyterian, Methodist); those Reformation churches with strict interpretations of their confessions (Missouri Synod Lutherans, Christian Reformed); the "peace" churches (Brethren, Mennonite, Friends); the more conservative wing of the Restoration movement (Campbellites); the "Holiness" tradition (Wesleyan Methodist); Baptists, the fundamentalist groups, which now include those who gather around radio or TV preachers, Pentecostals, most black churches; adherents of parachurch groups (the majority of U.S. Protestant mission organizations, Inter-Varsity Christian Fellowship, Campus Crusade for Christ, the Navigators, and so on). No wonder it is difficult to reach a description in which all the above would recognize themselves.[13]

Even so, just as Roman Catholics can be said to be in full communion with His Holiness John Paul II, regardless of their diversity, and just as Roman Catholics share a common set of beliefs, so too can that be said of Evangelicals. In spite of their seemingly endless variety, there is a tendency for them to exhibit at least three common characteristics: "a dedication to the gospel that is expressed in a personal faith in Christ as Lord, an understanding of the gospel as defined authoritatively by Scripture, and a desire to communicate the gospel both in evangelism and social reform."[14]

In this short definition of Evangelicals, we get a few clues about some basic differences between Catholics and Evangelicals. One of these has to do with the roles which Scripture and Tradition play within our respective movements. In this definition, Evangelicals are identified in part by their view that the Gospel is authoritatively defined by Scripture. Please notice, there is no mention of Tradition in this definition.

For Evangelicals to be so defined is not to argue that Roman Catholics do not embrace the authoritative role which Scripture plays in defining the Gospel. We know that this is not the case. But it does mean that the emphasis upon Tradition—even capital T Tradition—and the emphasis upon the role of any magisterium in interpreting Scripture or defining the Gospel will be different between Catholics and Evangelicals.

Evangelicals are suspicious of almost all tradition. They are frequently reluctant to grant authoritative space to what they perceive to be human action, even when that action might be called "Spirit-led" human action.[15] The one exception to this is the role which human beings may have played in the writing of Scripture, for Scripture carries with it the divine imprimatur of a claim to inspiration. Evangelicals believe that Scripture is quite literally "Godbreathed" (2 Tm 3:16), and they frequently point to the warning to beware of the *traditions* of human beings which they believe can lead them astray (cf. Col 2:8). As a result, Evangelicals generally do not distinguish between Tradition and tradition, but react negatively against any overt claim to the authority of tradition because they believe that it is subject to error.

A second part of this definition speaks of a dedication to the Gospel which is expressed in a "personal faith in Christ as Lord." Clearly, both Catholics and Evangelicals embrace Christ as Lord. But often at issue between Catholics and Evangelicals is the role of "personal faith," to say nothing of its content. Complicating matters even further is the relationship between "personal faith" and sacramental theology. Most Evangelicals are not sacramentalists, while Roman Catholics clearly are. While baptism serves as the sacramental mark of the moment of incorporation into the life of the Church within the Roman Catholic community, baptism is frequently understood only to be a symbolic act of obedience, an ordinance, to which Evangelicals submit at some point subsequent to their moment of conversion.[16] On the whole, Evangelicals tend to view entrance into the Church as occurring at the moment of conversion, a moment which they tend to express in the language of Jesus when He spoke to Nicodemus and told him that unless a person was "born again" (Jn 3:3, 7), that person would not see the kingdom of God. While there are Evangelicals who do baptize their infants, they tend to do so on the basis of a covenantal theology rather than a sacramental one. Even so, the majority of Evangelicals argue that a *personal* expression of faith in Christ must *precede* baptism, taking as their norm the New Testament model (cf. Acts 2:38; 8:12, 36–39; 10:34–48, etc.)[17] rather than from a model whose foundation they see as being derived from tradition.

In a sense, this part of the definition of Evangelicals raises questions surrounding the content of faith and the overall role of faith in the salvation process. I will not belabor the Reformation insistence upon a doctrine of "justification by faith alone," an issue on which significant progress has been made in recent years. But the issue of a "personal" faith is very much a point of contention, not because Roman Catholics necessarily lack personal faith, but because Evangelicals frequently interpret the idea of "personal" in individualistic terms, and Roman Catholics all too often find it difficult to *articulate* a personal faith in a passionate or convincing way.

For Evangelicals to place such a strong emphasis upon "personal" or "individual" faith without giving more care to the *corporate* nature of the Church is for them to miss a major ecclesiological point. One of the major weaknesses of Evangelicalism is its tendency toward individualism in faith and life. This begins with a real concern for "me and my relationship with Jesus" without an equally strong commitment to "me and my solidarity with my sisters and brothers in Christ." Baptism is clearly a point where such solidarity can be, and often is, proclaimed, but it does not carry the weight that it might otherwise convey, largely because of the fear that is expressed in Evangelical churches that people might believe that there is something magical or even salvific about the rite of baptism itself.[18]

For Roman Catholics to place such a strong emphasis upon the corporate sacrament of admission to the Church without placing an equally strong emphasis upon the acquisition of a *personal* relationship with Jesus is equally problematic, for it tends to produce Christians who are willing to rely upon membership in the Church as the means of salvation while taking upon themselves little or no personal responsibility. Thomas Weinandy, O.F.M. Cap., in an article titled "Why Catholics Should Witness Verbally to the Gospel," describes the situation as he sees it within the Catholic Church, as follows:

Many contemporary Catholics possess no evangelistic fervor. One reason could be that they have little or no experiential knowledge of Jesus, and may even be ignorant of the basic Gospel message: that Jesus himself is the Good News. Perhaps they simply have not been fully transformed by the power and life of the Holy Spirit that comes through faith in Jesus and thus are incapable of offering this new life to others.[19]

In this critique of Catholic experience, Weinandy sounds very much like an Evangelical. In another part of the same article he talks about a knowledge which is based upon "intellectual assent" to which he would seem to suggest that there is more.[20] There is also an experiential knowledge, or as one of my Jesuit friends recently told me, a *received* knowledge, to which one can add an *appropriated* knowledge. Evangelicals are concerned that Christians have both.

A third part of this definition carries this discussion one step further. Evangelicals are known for their "desire to communicate the Gospel both in evangelism and social reform." The emphasis here is on the *communication* of the Gospel much more than it is on the *means* of communication by either word or deed. Evangelicals are taught from the day they are "born again" to share their faith, proclaim the Gospel as best they can, and to bear witness to the One Who has saved them. Perhaps this accounts for their frequently aggressive and sometimes insensitive evangelistic fervor.[21]

On the other hand, it appears from the Evangelical perspective that Roman Catholics are typically not taught or not challenged to articulate their faith, to take any active part in the proclamation of the Gospel, or to bear any overt witness to the One Who has redeemed them. Even among those who do engage in evangelism within the Roman Catholic tradition, Fr. Weinandy has some major concerns. The first is what he calls "an excessive anxiety about getting the teaching right and extracting from the people merely intellectual assent...." The second is related to the desire to communicate the Gospel in various types of social reform. The trend he notes among many Roman Catholics who mean well in this regard is what he calls their "…inordinate concern for the legitimate issues of justice, peace, or freedom which, especially when divorced from the person of Christ, become a new moralism." It is a confusion of personal, cultural, or political agendas, in short, the confusion with the "cultural clothing of Western society," even the confusion of charitable works with evangelization.[22]

What all of this suggests, then, is that in many areas of faith and practice Evangelicals and Roman Catholics do not see things from the same perspective. Yet even in our differences, there are gifts and correctives that we can bring to one another. As His Holiness John Paul II has noted in his recent encyclical *Ut Unum Sint,* Christian unity is nor merely "a matter of adding together all the riches scattered throughout the various Christian Communities in order to arrive at a Church which God has in mind for the future," for there is an *already* character to the Church which is derived from the Pentecost event.[23]

If in fact Evangelicals and Roman Catholics are on the one hand so different, and yet on the other so much alike, what key events have made possible the state of the discussion of Evangelicals and Roman Catholics at the present time? In what ways have Evangelicals and Roman Catholics already started their life together?

## ◆◆    DEVELOPMENTS IN CATHOLICISM    ◆◆

There are a number of events which have contributed to greater understanding and cooperation between Roman Catholics and Evangelicals during this century. I will mention only two of them. The first of these is clearly the Second Vatican Council. Where would we be without the fresh wind of the Spirit that blew through Rome in the early 1960s? We need only to be reminded of the words of Pope Pius XI in his encyclical *Mortalium Animos* to recognize how far apart we were. In that 1928 encyclical he wrote that he was opposed to any move toward unity among the churches which did not begin in Rome, "for the union of Christians can only be promoted by promoting the return to the one true Church of

Christ of those who are separated from it, for in the past they have unhappily left it." He went on to announce that the "Spouse of Christ has never been contaminated...." Thus the clear message to Protestants, as well as to Roman Catholics who were looking longingly at the initiatives toward greater unity and cooperation between the churches other than the Roman Catholic Church, was that the Protestants alone had sinned by separating themselves from Rome at the time of the Reformation, and if they were to be reconciled at all, it would be completely on Roman terms.[24]

The Second Vatican Council brought with it a new way of doing business, best described by Pope John XXIII's choice of the word *aggiornamento,* which meant "updating," "modernization," or "adaptation." This new way of doing business and the signal events which accompanied it pointed toward new possibilities within the larger Church. And Evangelicals were watching. When the bishops wrote in the *Dogmatic Constitution on the Church* that as they looked beyond the confines of the Roman Catholic Church they had identified in other places "many elements of sanctification and of truth," Evangelicals were pleased.[25] When the bishops penned the *Decree on Ecumenism* and admitted, perhaps for the first time, that "men on both sides were to blame" for the separation which had occurred at the time of the Reformation, and that it was inappropriate to view those persons who were outside the Roman Catholic Church as in some way necessarily guilty of the sins of their forebears, Evangelicals were surprised.[26] When in that same document the bishops suggested that the appropriate title for believers who were not Roman Catholic was "brothers," since "men who believe in Christ and have been properly baptized are put in some, though imperfect communion with the Catholic Church," Evangelicals decided that they needed to look more carefully at what was going on.[27] When the bishops elaborated on the need for missionary activity, the necessity for faith and baptism and the unique mediatorial role of Jesus Christ in their *Decree on the Church's Missionary Activity,* Evangelicals heartily agreed.[28] When the bishops declared in their *Decree on the Apostolate of Lay People* that "a member [of the Church] who does not work at the growth of the body to the extent of his possibilities must be considered *useless* both to the Church and to himself,"[29] Evangelicals must have thought that it was about time! And when the bishops challenged its members in the *Decree on Ecumenism* to greater faithfulness in their Christian walk by noting that although they had been "endowed with all divinely revealed truth and with all means of grace," they nonetheless "fail[ed] to live by them with all the fervor they should," and then went on to contend that "every Catholic must therefore aim at Christian perfection...,"[30] Evangelicals could practically hear the strains of the hymn "Just As I Am Without One Plea."

The second major event which caused a variety of Evangelicals to take another look at the Roman Catholic Church was the rise of the Charismatic Renewal. As part of the larger Evangelical Movement, Pentecostals had prayed since the turn of the century for an outpouring of the Holy Spirit on all flesh according to Joel 2:28–30. It was difficult enough for them to accept it when such an outpouring of the Holy Spirit began to take place within Protestant churches in 1959, but when it began to happen within the Roman Catholic Church it blew all of their preprogrammed circuits. As Doug Wead wrote in his 1972 book *Father McCarthy Smokes a Pipe and Speaks in Tongues*,[31] Pentecostals asked themselves, "How could this be?" The Spirit was supposed to come upon people who lived a *holy* life, a sanctified life, and if one smoked, one was clearly not living a holy life.

When other writers such as Rene Laurentin lifted up "Mary, Model of the Charismatic," Pentecostals again worried aloud.[32] When other Roman Catholics began to testify how their faith was deepened, how they now had a greater reverence for the Eucharist, how they were now regularly reading the Bible, and how their charismatic experience had contributed to a rising devotion to Mary, Pentecostals were torn again. On the one hand, they saw some good things. On the other, they could not understand how any charismatic experience could increase devotion to Mary.

At first, Roman Catholic leadership was troubled by the emergence of the Charismatic Renewal in its midst. It sounded too much like Pentecostalism to them, and admittedly some Catholic

Charismatics left the Roman Catholic Church to join Pentecostal and other Evangelical congregations, while other Catholic Charismatics tended not to want to submit to their local bishops who were themselves not sure whether they should even tolerate the Renewal in their dioceses. Today, the Renewal claims to have a membership of at least 60,000,000, has an office in Vatican City which publishes a bi-monthly newsletter,[33] and enjoys the blessing of bishops and the pope alike.

The rapid and enormous growth of Pentecostals worldwide, which (in Latin America at least) comprises in some countries as much as 85 percent of all those classed as Evangelicals, is a wonder to behold.[34] It is little wonder that the Vatican should take an intense interest in this part of the Evangelical world. The number of persons transferring from their Roman Catholic parish to some Pentecostal or Evangelical church each year is staggering. In a 1993 article carried by the *Los Angeles Times,* James Brooke noted that about 600,000 Catholics a year are leaving their churches in Brazil alone. Many of them are showing up in Evangelical churches.[35] When we take the total number of Pentecostals and Charismatics together, as does statistician David B. Barrett, we see that as of January 2000 there were 523,767,000 such persons in the world, comprising the second largest and fastest-growing Christian movement in the world.[36] The Pentecostal movement is alive and doing well, often at Catholic expense.

◆◆     SOME TENTATIVE STEPS     ◆◆

Beginning in 1969 and continuing through 1971, the Vatican explored with Pentecostal minister, David duPlessis, the possibility of establishing an ongoing international Dialogue between the Roman Catholic Church and members of the Pentecostal Movement. That Dialogue was formally launched in 1972, and in 1997 completed its fourth major period of study. Between 1972 and 1979, it was a time of getting acquainted. Because the Charismatic Renewal was still relatively young in the Roman Catholic Church, a number of the topics which were discussed revolved around various charismatic phenomena.

In the second round of discussions (1977–1982) the gloves came off, and more difficult issues were placed on the agenda, issues like Scripture and Tradition, exegesis and the interpretation of the Bible, faith and reason, healing in the Church, ministry in the Church, and even the topic of Mary. During the third quinquennium of study (1985–1989), the Dialogue focused its attention on the topic of *koinonia*, sometimes translated as "fellowship," but encompassing a number of issues from the communion of saints to life in the Church. Of particular interest was the surprising convergence reached on the subject of baptism.

Perhaps of most significance has been the series of topics which preoccupied the attention of the International Dialogue from 1991–1997. It is of great significance precisely because it is exploring sensitive territory, the whole arena of evangelism, and evangelization. The two sides have explored their respective biblical and theological bases for mission and evangelism, and found remarkable agreement. They have exchanged their histories of mission. They have explored issues which have emerged as a result of the increasing role of secularization, especially in Europe, but now very much in evidence within the United States. They have engaged one another in tough questions about the role of culture in preparing people for evangelism, as well as the dangers to evangelism which some cultures raise. They have talked about syncretism and how far it is acceptable. But perhaps most strongly, they have engaged one another on the relationship between evangelization and proselytism. This, more than any other single issue, has demanded their attention, and the Dialogue team members are hopeful that their statement, "Evangelization, Proselytism and Common Witness" adds a new dimension to this often difficult and frequently painful dimension of our common Christian lives together.[37]

Beginning in 1977, and completing its work in 1984, was a second dialogue conducted by the Pontifical Council (then the Secretariat) for Promoting Christian Unity and non-Pentecostal

Evangelicals. It came about, in part, because of Evangelical interest in Pope Paul VI's 1975 letter on evangelism, *Evangelii Nuntiandi,* and in part as a result of the recently-concluded International Congress on World Evangelization which had convened in Lausanne, Switzerland in 1974. Like the participants in the Pentecostal Dialogue, the Evangelical participants in this Dialogue on Mission did not come as official representatives of any denomination, or even of the World Evangelical Fellowship or the Lausanne Continuation Committee. They came as individuals who were interested in developing greater understanding between Roman Catholics and Evangelicals while discussing a topic which was very important to both sides. What resulted from this discussion was a report which, as the editors noted, was not an "agreed statement," but rather a description of a number of commonly held views which emerged as they spent time together. It consists of seven major sections which give some hint as to what was discussed. They include (1) Revelation and Authority, (2) The Nature of Mission, (3) The Gospel of Salvation, (4) Our Response in the Holy Spirit to the Gospel, (5) The Church and the Gospel, (6) The Gospel and Culture, and (7) The Possibilities of Common Witness.[38] Not surprisingly, the Pentecostal discussion of 1991–1997 included some of these same basic themes.

Since 1991, the Vatican has made further contact with the World Evangelical Fellowship,[39] and in 1993 a new round of discussions was undertaken, beginning with the topics of Scripture, Tradition, and Justification by Faith. The Catholic Church in the United States has also been engaged in a conversation with the Southern Baptist Convention.

It is these kinds of officially sanctioned encounters which have led His Eminence Cardinal Edward I. Cassidy, president of the Pontifical Council for Promoting Christian Unity, to make the following affirmation before a gathering of the representatives of the National Episcopal Commissions for Ecumenism in May, 1993. He noted:

> We must be careful, however, not to confuse the issue [of sects and new religious movements] by lumping together, under

the term "sect," groups that do not deserve that title. I am not speaking here, for instance, about the evangelical movement among Protestants, nor about Pentecostalism as such. The Pontifical Council has had fruitful dialogue and significant contacts with certain evangelical groups and with Pentecostals. Indeed, one can speak of a mutual enrichment as a result of these contacts.[40]

◆◆     A COMMON FUTURE?     ◆◆

A series of recent articles which are raising questions about the future of ecumenism have pointed to the fact that Catholics, Evangelicals, and Pentecostals are not at the forefront of either the National Council of Churches in this country or in the World Council of Churches. It is true that the Catholic Church has membership in the Commission on Faith and Order of both organizations, but there are few Evangelical groups which can claim even this and very few Evangelicals from member churches who believe that their concerns are fairly represented by these denominational leaders. It is safe to say that the national Council is not truly national when Catholics and Evangelicals are not present or are inadequately represented.

It is equally safe to say that the World Council of Churches is not fully representative of the Church around the world when the two largest Christian movements in the world, the Roman Catholic Church and the Pentecostals, to say nothing of the larger Evangelical Movement, are not members. Father O. C. Edwards, an Episcopal priest, has summarized the work of the ecclesiology study group of Faith and Order in the NCC between 1991 and 1995 and suggests that the NCC think about what he calls "The Far Horizon of Ecumenism: Roman Catholics, Evangelicals and Pentecostals as Potential Partners with the National Council of Churches."[41]

More recently, the American Baptist professor of theology at Andover Newton Theological School, S. Mark Heim, has suggested that the NCC and WCC look to what he calls "The Next Ecumenical Movement." Noting the problems of both organizations, their lack of meeting their goals, their financial predicaments, their declining vision and membership, Professor Heim observes that "The most dynamic growth is elsewhere—among Pentecostals, Roman Catholics, Southern Baptists and independent churches."[42] He suggests that the survival of ecumenism depends upon the inclusion of those who have traditionally been absent from the table, including Roman Catholics and Evangelicals of all stripes.

Evangelicals appear to share with Roman Catholics more beliefs and views in common than Evangelicals share with the liberal wing of Protestantism. Together, Evangelicals and Catholics share a commitment to Scripture which is often not reflected in other areas of Protestantism. They share a commitment to the reality of the Virgin Birth, the reality of sin, the need for salvation which is available only through what God has done in Christ Jesus, to the necessity of faith in the process of salvation, to the need for conversion, indeed, for multiple conversions or rededications. They are not afraid to go to God and ask for healing. Many Evangelicals, and especially Pentecostals, as well as Roman Catholics still believe in the reality of miracles today. They believe in the reality of heaven and hell, in the judgment yet to come, in the resurrection of the body, and in the bodily return of Jesus from heaven. Indeed, I suspect that they hold much more in common than that on which they disagree. This claim can be made, however, without denying the gravity of the things over which they still disagree.

Father Avery Dulles, S. J., has summoned Roman Catholics to explore a new alignment in what he calls "an ecumenism of mutual enrichment." The time is ripe, he argues,

> to welcome the more traditional and conservative churches into the dialogue. For the Catholic Church it may not prove easy to reach a consensus with either the Orthodox or the conservative evangelicals, but these churches and communities may have more to offer than some others because they have dared to be different. Catholics have the right and duty to challenge the adequacy of some of their positions, but they should be invited to challenge Catholics in their turn.[43]

I think that this challenge can be met not only at the international and national levels, but also on the local level, especially if we follow a few basic guidelines. Let me suggest seven such guidelines for consideration.

1. We must know our own traditions and be able to look at them with an objective eye, willing to acknowledge both strengths and weaknesses. This is frequently difficult for any of us to do, since all of our training within our respective traditions is spent in helping us see what is right about us and wrong about the other. We need to be honest and admit that all of us are flawed, and that all of us are something of the genius of God.

2. We must be willing to try to understand one another from *the other's perspective,* rather than merely our own perspective. Again, this is difficult to do because we are used to seeing things our own way. But I suggest that this act, as much as anything, will help us to break down preconceived notions and long-nourished stereotypes. There is nothing like spending time together and listening to one another in a genuine attempt to get into each other's shoes that will ultimately help us gain a greater understanding and appreciation for one another.

3. We must be willing to compare strength for strength and weakness for weakness and to admit it when we have violated this standard. Once again, this is a very difficult task. We are not used to doing this. But it seems to me to be only fair. It is very easy for us to proclaim our strengths and curse the weaknesses of others but, without parity in the process, we run the risk of slandering one another or contributing to the bearing of false witness about one another instead of recognizing that we are both strong and flawed, and that we are attempting to serve the same Lord Jesus Christ.

4. Together we can approach the Scriptures and ask what they say to our situation, if anything. I believe that this can be done without violating our confessional patterns; that is, Catholics need not deviate from magisterial teaching, and Evangelicals need not deviate from a position which allows both personal and communal attempts at exegesis. Whatever way it

happens, it must be done openly and honestly with all presuppositions on the table.

5. We need to be careful not to make premature or inappropriate judgments about one another, especially about the motives which we think the other might have for wanting the discussion in the first place. I recognize that this is a place where we risk some things, but within the Pentecostal community, as well as the remainder of the Evangelical community, there are many who fail at this point. They ascribe motives to Roman Catholics who look forward to dialogue with Evangelicals who are reminiscent of the pronouncement of Pope Pius XI that any such conversation is a devious attempt to get Evangelicals back into the arms of Rome. But frequently they fail to assess their own motives for attempting to persuade Catholics to leave their own churches and join Evangelical ones.

It seems to me that sooner or later we must recognize that like all things which we do in our Christian walk, the pursuit of genuine understanding, to say nothing of unity, requires both honesty and risktaking. Not to ascribe preconceived motives is an act of trust, an act of faith in the One who has called us as sisters and brothers to share at the one table. It would be a shame to miss the opportunity to do so, simply because we presume that the other partner cannot be trusted.

6. We need to avoid any willingness to compromise for the sake of some presumed level of unity. Genuine unity often comes even when we disagree profoundly over an issue, but we agree to disagree. This search for greater unity between us, for visible manifestations of unity between us, is like a marriage. We will not agree on everything. We are entitled to our own opinions. Any attempt not to recognize this, or to smooth over differences as though they do not exist, is not helpful. We need to know where the rocks are. We need to be honest about our differences. People in dialogue with one another must know who they are and what they believe. They cannot be people who are prone to "spiritual

insecurity," for that is what ultimately breeds compromise, and compromise results in a false sense of unity.

7. Finally, we need to be open to the surprises which God might have in store for us, even up to and including what we might now be willing to call a new reality. I have already mentioned the dreams of Father O. C. Edwards and the National Council of Churches. I have mentioned, too, the dreams of Professor Mark Heim for the World Council of Churches. I have noted the proposal of Father Avery Dulles for an "ecumenism of mutual enrichment." In the 1940s, many people within the historic churches thought that the World Council of Churches would be the means of bringing about visible unity between all churches.

That hope was given a new burst of energy during and immediately following the Second Vatican Council. Now we are hearing suggestions that the World Council and its churches are in major difficulty, and there are some who are even suggesting that it may not survive in its present form. To be quite honest, we do not know what form our life together as Christians will take in the future. But we must be willing to enter the future together with faith in the One who has called us to oneness, even as He and the Father are One (Jn 17:21–22).

◆◆　　CONCLUSION　　◆◆

If I could emphasize just one point, it would be the need for Evangelicals and Roman Catholics to get to know one another. It is in the day-to-day life, in table talk, in dialogue, in personal sharing where the stereotypes will be dealt with, the fears will begin to dissipate, and real differences can be settled. If we are not there yet, perhaps we can at least pause to pray together. There is something that is particularly humbling about kneeling at the foot of the cross before our common Lord and Savior, Jesus Christ. In that act, at the foot of the cross, love is manifested.

In summary, I find the words of Pope John Paul II, in his encyclical *Ut Unum Sint,* to be an especially good reminder of what love is all about. He writes:

Love is the great undercurrent which gives life and adds vigor to the movement towards unity. This love *finds its most complete expression in common prayer.* When brothers and sisters who are not in perfect communion with one another come together to pray, the Second Vatican Council defines their prayer *as the soul of the whole ecumenical movement.* The prayer is "a very effective means of petitioning for the grace of unity," *"a genuine expression of the ties which even now bind Catholics to their separated brethren."* Even when prayer is not specifically offered for Christian unity, but for other intentions such as peace, it actually becomes an expression and a confirmation of unity. The common prayer of Christians is an invitation to Christ himself to visit the community of those who call upon him: "Where two or three are gathered in my name, there am I in the midst of them" (Mt 18:20). [Italics added].[44]

## Notes

1. "Evangelicals and Catholics Together: The Christian Mission in the Third Millennium," *First Things* No. 43 (May 1994), 15–22.

2. "Catholics and Evangelicals in the Trenches," *Christianity Today,* 38:6 (May 1994), 16–17.

3. Common cause is often found on issues such as the right to life, religious freedom, and parental choice in education.

4. John Paul II, *Ut Unum Sint* (Vatican City: Libreria Editrice Vaticana, 1995), no. 79.

5. Former Assemblies of God minister, Jimmy Swaggart, spoke for many Evangelicals as well as Pentecostals when he declared that there was a vast gap between Catholicism and Christianity in his book *Catholicism & Christianity* (Baton Rouge, La.: Jimmy Swaggart Ministries, 1986).

6. Terry Peretti, "Learning from the Past, Looking to the Future," *The Pentecostal Evangel* 4220 (March 26, 1995) 19.

7. Elizabeth Altham, "Protestant Pastors on the Road to Rome," *Sursum Corda,* Special Promotional Edition, no date [1996], 2–13.

8. Cardinal Ernesto Corripio Ahumada, *Regional Report on North America April 5, 1991, in Sects and New Religious Movements.*

*An Anthology of Texts from the Catholic Church 1986–1994* (Washington, D.C.: United States Catholic Conference, 1995), 4.

9. George M. Marsden, *Fundamentalism and American Culture: The Shaping of Twentieth-Century Evangelicalism 1870–1925* (Oxford: Oxford University Press, 1980).

10. George M. Marsden, *Reforming Fundamentalism: Fuller Seminary and the New Evangelicalism* (Grand Rapids, Mich.: William B. Eerdmans Publishing Company, 1987).

11. Donald W. Dayton, "'The Search for the Historical Evanglicalism': George Marsden's History of Fuller Seminary as a Case Study," *Christian Scholar's Review* 23:1 (1992), 12–33.

12. Cf. Donald W. Dayton, "Yet Another Layer of the Onion: Or Opening the Ecumenical Door to Let the Riffraff In," *Ecumenical Review* 40:1 (January 1988), 87–110.

13. Thomas F. Stransky, "A Look at Evangelical Protestantism," *Theology News & Notes* 35:1 (March 1988), 24.

14. Robert K. Johnston, "American Evangelicalism: An Extended Family," in Donald W. Dayton and Robert K. Johnston, *The Variety of American Evangelicalism* (Knoxville, Tenn.: The University of Tennessee Press, 1991), 261.

15. Harold Lindsell's *The Battle for the Bible* (Grand Rapids, Mich.: Zondervan, 1976) and his sequel, *The Bible in the Balance* (Grand Rapids, Mich.: Zondervan, 1979) are two examples of books written from within the Evangelical community which suggest this concern.

16. For the example of the Pentecostal community which has clear links to a more broadly defined Evangelicalism, see Cecil M. Robeck, Jr., and Jerry L. Sandidge, "The Ecclesiology of *Koinonia* and Baptism: A Pentecostal Perspective," *Journal of Ecumenical Studies* 27:3 (Summer, 1990), 519.

17. See, for example, "Perspectives on *Koinonia*: The Report from the Third Quinquennium of the Dialogue between the Pontifical Council for Promoting Christian Unity of the Roman Catholic Church and some Classical Pentecostal Churches and Leaders 1989," Paragraphs 42–47, in *Pneuma: The Journal of the Society for Pentecostal Studies* 12:2 (Fall, 1990), 126–127.

18. Cf. Robeck and Sandidge, "The Ecclesiology of *Koinonia* and Baptism," 516.

19. Thomas Weinandy, "Why Catholics Should Witness Verbally to the Gospel," *New Oxford Review* 60:6 (July–August 1993), 16.

20. Ibid., 17.

21. Cecil M. Robeck, Jr., "Taking Stock of Pentecostalism: The Personal Reflections of a Retiring Editor," *Pneuma: The Journal of the Society for Pentecostal Studies* 15:1 (Spring 1993), 51–58, esp. 51–52.

22. Weinandy, "Why Catholics Should Witness," 17.

23. John Paul II, *Ut Unum Sint*, no. 14.

24. Pope Pius XI, *Mortalium Animos*, in Claudia Carlen, *The Papal Encyclicals 1903–1939* (Wilmington, N.C.: McGrath Publishing Co., 1981), 317.

25. *Dogmatic Constitution on the Church (Lumen gentium)*, no. 8. All quotations from documents originating in the Second Vatican Council are from Austin Flannery, ed. *Vatican II: The Conciliar and Post Conciliar Documents* (Collegeville, Minn.: The Liturgical Press, 1975, revised 1984).

26. *Decree on Ecumenism (Unitatis Redintegratio)*, no. 3.

27. *Decree on Ecumenism*, no. 3.

28. *Decree on the Church's Missionary Activity (Ad Gentes Divinitus)*, nos. 1–7.

29. *Decree on the Apostolate of Lay People (Apostolicam Actuositatem)*, no. 2.

30. *Decree on Ecumenism*, no. 4.

31. R. Douglas Wead, *Father McCarthy Smokes a Pipe and Speaks in Tongues* (Norfolk, Va.: Wisdom House, 1972).

32. Rene Laurentin, "Mary, Model of the Charismatic as Seen in Acts 1–2, Luke 1–2, and John," in Vincent P. Branick, *Mary, the Spirit and the Church* (Mahwah, N.J.: Paulist Press, 1980), 28–43.

33. The International Catholic Charismatic Renewal Services publishes the *ICCRS Newsletter* and has its offices at Palazzo della Cancelleria, 00120,Vatican City.

34. It is difficult to get precise figures on the number of Pentecostals in Latin America, and figures can be deceiving. Still, Edward L. Cleary has recently contended that 75–90 percent of contemporary Protestant growth in Latin America is Pentecostal growth. See Edward L. Cleary, "Introduction: Pentecostals, Prominence, and Politics," in Edward L. Cleary and Hannah W. Stewart-Gambino, eds., *Power, Politics and Pentecostals in Latin America* (Boulder, Colo.: Westview Press, 1974) 3–4.

35. James Brooke, "Protestant Gains Dramatic, High-tech through Brazil" (*Los Angeles Times* July 17, 1993), A 12.

36. David B. Barrett, "Annual Statistical Table on Global Mission: 2000," *International Bulletin of Missionary Research* 24:1 (January 2000), 24–25.

37. Pentecostal Roman Catholic International Dialogue, "Evangelization, Proselytism and Common Witness," *Information Service*, 97 I–II (1998), 38–56; see also *Pneuma: The Journal of the Society for Pentecostal Studies* 21:1 (Spring 1999), 11–51.

38. Basil Meeking and John Stott, eds. *The Evangelical Roman Catholic Dialogue on Mission 1977–1984: A Report* (Grand Rapids, Mich.: William B. Eerdmans, 1986).

39. "Relationships with Evangelicals," *Information Service* 91 (1996/I–II), 44.

40. Edward Idris Cardinal Cassidy, "Prolusio," *Information Service* 84 (1993/III–IV), 122.

41. O. C. Edwards, Jr., "The Far Horizon of Ecumenism: Roman Catholics, Evangelicals and Pentecostals as Potential Partners with the National Council of Churches," *Ecumenical Trends* 25:2 (February 1996), 7–29.

42. S. Mark Heim, "The Next Ecumenical Movement," *The Christian Century* 113: 24 (August 14–21, 1996), 780.

43. Avery Dulles, *The Craft of Theology: From Symbol to System* (New York, N.Y.: Crossroad, 1992), 193.

44. John Paul II, *Ut Unum Sint*, no 21.

# Catholic-Evangelical Relations:
# Signs of Progress

*Thomas P. Rausch*

Relations between Catholics and Evangelical Christians histori-
cally have not been close. American Protestantism was largely evangelical until the triumph of liberal Protestantism in the twentieth
century. Since Vatican II Catholics have generally been more comfortable with Protestants from the so-called "mainline" churches, those
established traditions stemming from the sixteenth-century Reformation, each with a clear sense of its own ecclesial and theological identity and its own historical relationship to the Catholic Church.

Evangelicals are more difficult for Catholics to categorize.
First, modern Evangelical Christianity appeared at some distance

from Catholicism, emerging as it did out of a number of evangelical revivals within eighteenth- and nineteenth-century Protestantism—Pietism within German Lutheranism, Wesley's Methodist movement within the Church of England, and the "Great Awakening" within early American Protestantism. Second, Evangelical Christianity is pluralistic, embracing a wide variety of Evangelicals as well as Pentecostals and fundamentalists. Some are members of historic churches, some belong to Evangelical or Pentecostal churches and congregations, others are non-denominational Christians. In the United States many of them are conservative "Establishment Evangelicals" who constitute a large percentage of the "religious right" represented by groups such as the Christian Coalition, founded by Pat Robertson.[1] Others are "New Evangelicals" whose Christian witness includes a practical concern for the social implications of the Gospel. The Sojourners community and the Church of the Savior, both in Washington, D.C., are representative of this group. Some Evangelical theologians show in their writings the social and economic dimensions of God's saving and liberating grace. But what is common to all Evangelicals is a "born again" or conversion experience establishing an affective relationship with Jesus as one's personal Lord and Savior, an insistence on the sufficiency of Scripture *(sola Scriptura),* and an urgency for bringing the saving word of the Gospel to others.

Evangelicals have often been deeply suspicious of Catholics. Many have argued that Catholicism is a false religion, teaching works righteousness instead of justification by faith alone, substituting the Church for the Lord, encouraging non-biblical practices such as veneration of Mary and the saints. Pentecostals dislike the formalism of worship in the liturgical churches, seeing it as a substitution for the vitality of the Spirit. They are profoundly suspicious of the historical-critical theological methodologies used by Catholics and mainline Protestants. Since many of them consider baptized Catholics as being among the unsaved, they have made them the object of their evangelizing efforts, and with considerable success. Millions of Hispanic Catholics in Latin America and the United States have joined Evangelical and especially Pentecostal churches.[2]

Catholics have often tended to stereotype Evangelicals and Pentecostals. Without bothering to distinguish the varieties of evangelical Christianity, they have tended to dismiss all Evangelicals as fundamentalists. Even the Vatican has failed to distinguish between Evangelical and Pentecostal churches and groups such as the Mormons and the Jehovah's Witnesses, lumping them all together in its official documents under the term "sects." Many of the former were deeply offended when Pope John Paul II in his remarks at the Fourth General Conference of Latin American Bishops (CELAM), held at Santo Domingo in 1992, implicitly included them among the "sects" which he characterized as acting like "rapacious wolves," devouring Latin American Catholics and "causing division and discord" in Catholic communities.[3]

In Latin America, relations between Catholics and Protestants have deteriorated to the point that the governing board for the Latin American Council of Churches (CLAI) decided not to invite official representatives of the Catholic Church to its Third General Assembly in Concepción, Chile, in late January 1995 because of worsening relations between Catholics and Protestants throughout the continent. According to Protestant theologian José Míguez-Bonino, the Catholic Church is moving from the positions it espoused at the time of Vatican II to a "neo-Christendom," and many express concern over the Vatican's policy of naming conservatives to replace progressive and ecumenically-minded bishops.[4] Others object that Catholic bishops in many Latin American countries continue to insist that only Catholicism be taught in the state-supported schools, in spite of the presence of students from other churches. As the Episcopal bishop of Mexico City has said, the Catholic Church in Mexico has a "superiority complex": "It is the Church of the majority, and therefore it feels that there is no reason to take the other Churches into consideration."[5]

Evangelicals and Pentecostals have generally been slow to embrace the ecumenical movement. Many fear that drawing closer to other churches would mean a blurring of doctrinal differences, and they often misunderstand the goal of ecumenism as implying some kind of institutional superchurch, an anathema to the individualism of so many Evangelicals. Most Evangelical and Pentecostal churches have refused to take part in the World Council of Churches, considering its agenda as more social-political than religious; they see "spiritual" unity as more biblical.[6] Many Southern Baptists, who see the true church as spiritual and invisible, will argue that ecumenism has never been part of the mission of the Baptist churches.

◆◆    SIGNS OF PROGRESS    ◆◆

In recent years, however, there have been some significant signs of progress. On the international level some dialogues have been initiated. The first formal meeting of the Pentecostal-Roman Catholic Dialogue took place in 1972.[7] An Evangelical-Roman Catholic Dialogue on Mission was established in 1977.[8] However official dialogue is difficult. Catholics are challenged to find new ways of relating to dialogue partners who represent "streams" or "movements" rather than clear ecclesial traditions.[9] The participants from these movements are not official representatives of any international body and are not always supported by their communities. Neither the Pentecostal World Conference nor the national Pentecostal Fellowship of North America has supported the Pentecostal-Roman Catholic Dialogue, so some participants must come on their own. Yet as Peter Hocken has pointed out, "the greater vitality" of these "non-ecumenicals," in contrast to the mainline or "ecumenical" traditions, "suggests that the ecumenical movement, at least in its more institutional expressions, has somehow lost touch with the most dynamic currents of revival and renewal."[10]

Dialogues are important. But there can be no real ecumenical progress until Christians in local congregations begin to recognize each other as sharing a common faith and thus as brothers and sisters in the Lord. Thus what is particularly significant in relations between Evangelical-Pentecostal Christians and Catholics are the new relationships presently being formed at the grass roots. In what is a surprising development to many ecumenists, representatives of these traditions are beginning to recognize the number of concerns they share in common, among them strengthening the family, the welfare of children, the sanctity of life, the place of religious values in society, and—most importantly—evangelization. Even more significantly, they are beginning to cooperate in ways which only a few years ago would have seemed impossible. Some examples.

## Youth and Renewal Ministries

Evangelicals are effective communicators; as Peter Hocken says, "their distinctive witness to the Spirit lies primarily in the areas of conversion-evangelization, discipleship training, congregational planting, and spiritual empowerment."[11] They have been particularly successful in working with young people through ministries such as Young Life, Campus Crusade for Christ, and Inter-Varsity Fellowship. Unfortunately, the often negative evaluation of the Catholic Church by these groups has made most Catholics hesitant to try and work with them. In parishes, Catholic youth ministers have for years watched in frustration while young Catholics who showed little interest in their programs would accompany their non-Catholic friends to Young Life meetings at a near-by Protestant church.

College campus ministers have objected that groups like Inter-Varsity Fellowship and Campus Crusade for Christ have often tended to work in competition with the historic churches and in fact are often anti-ecclesial, setting up independent fellowships, sometimes with non-denominational sacramental rituals. Few campus ministers at Catholic institutions have been open to welcoming these groups to their campuses. One campus minister told me that at his campus, a private non-Catholic college, Inter-Varsity Fellowship sponsored an "ecumenical" afternoon of prayer and fellowship at the university pool. At the end of an afternoon of testimonies and exhortation, one of the team said, "Well, we have a pool here; what is to prevent us from celebrating baptism for those who want to give themselves to the Lord?" It sounded spontaneous, but in fact this non-denominational baptism had all been carefully planned in advance.

In the last few years, however, there have been signs of a new sensitivity to Catholics in some of these groups and they have begun to work with Catholic pastors and youth ministers rather than in competition with them. As early as 1975 in Poland, Father Franzciszek Blachnicki, founder of the Light-Life Movement, recognized the effectiveness of Evangelical Protestants in evangelization and began a close collaboration with Campus Crusade for Christ.[12] Since then, Campus Crusade has been exploring other possible ways of participating with established churches in church renewal. An internal Campus Crusade report on European missions describes a number of signs of new life within European churches.[13] In Florence a Campus Crusade for Christ team was having limited success working with Catholics, since for them renewal meant joining a Protestant church. But when they met a Bible study group from a Catholic parish, they were impressed and changed their approach. After an initial presentation to a group from the parish, the parish priest invited them to begin a women's Bible study and later on to work with the parish youth. Their ministry in cooperation with the parish staff now touches hundreds of families.

The report also speaks highly of Alpha-Omega, an officially recognized lay Roman Catholic movement for the evangelization of Italy. With staffs in Rome, Modena, and Verona, Alpha-Omega trains teams which do direct evangelization in parishes under the supervision of the local priest. It uses a book based on Campus Crusade's "Four Spiritual Laws" to present the Gospel to parish families. The report urges this model of evangelization, working through the local parish and parish priest, as a model for Italy and other European countries. It praises the openness of the Catholic Church to Bible teaching and argues that Protestants and Catholics can work together in this "ecumenical" ministry, even if this occasions some "criticism from well-meaning relatives, friends and colleagues" for working with Catholics.

Peter Hocken tells a similar story of the Evangelical para-church agency, Youth With a Mission (YWAM). Founded in the late 1950s, the members of YWAM shared the belief that Catholics were not real Christians until Bruce Clewett, a young American working in Poland, began to ask if it really helped young Poles to attempt to draw them out of their own Catholic culture and tradition and turn them into westernized Protestants. His realization that Catholics could stay in their churches, arrived at after two years of prayer, led to a gradual change in YWAM which today cooperates with Catholics in Malta, Ghana, Uganda, Austria, and the Philippines. In Ireland, the YWAM staff as of 1994 was 75 percent Catholic.[14]

One of the most successful Evangelical ministries to adolescents is Young Life. In recent years Young Life has been seeking to develop its ministry in partnership with local congregations, and has made efforts to cooperate more effectively with Catholics. Bishop Richard Hanifen of Colorado Springs served on Young Life's Church Relations Advisory Council for a number of years and has taken part in some of their national conferences on Christian leadership. His diocese has entered a partnership with Young Life.

An internal Young Life document entitled *The Church and Young Life: Partners in Ministry* has a special section on "Ministering To and With Catholic Young People," written by Dan Ponsetto, a Catholic campus minister at Boston College. Its purpose is to help Protestant youth ministers understand the different religious culture of young Catholics by explaining the experience of faith from a Catholic perspective, including the meaning of sacramental reconciliation, the centrality of the Eucharist, Catholic teaching on Mary and the saints, a proper understanding of the papacy and its authority, and the differences between the Catholic and Protestant biblical canon. Particularly effective is its discussion of the different languages that Protestants and Catholics use to describe conversion. It stresses that for Catholics, conversion is seen as a life-long process. Hence it is confusing or even insulting to talk to a young Catholic about becoming a Christian when he or she has been involved for years in weekly worship, religious education, retreats, and has made a conscious decision to receive the sacrament of confirmation.[15]

Unfortunately, as several Young Life staffers admitted to me, this kind of openness does not characterize all Young Life groups, just as there are many Catholic dioceses which want nothing to do with Young Life or other Evangelical parachurch groups.

But there is also much promise. Ponsetto's guide, written in 1991, is still being circulated in varying degrees within Young Life. In some parts of the country Young Life and Catholics are working together in collaborative programs for training youth ministers. One Young Life director who had been working closely with representatives of the National Federation of Catholic Youth Directors commented on how much Young Life was learning from the Catholic Church's liturgical tradition and from its commitment to social justice. If Evangelical outreach agencies such as Campus Crusade for Christ, YWAM, and Young Life were to bring their zeal and Evangelical skills to the renewal of Catholic parishes, it could be a significant contribution to building up the body of Christ. Later in this book, David Bjork, an Evangelical pastor will describe his experience of working with Catholic communities in France over the last twenty years.

One of the most rapidly growing Evangelical renewal movements is Promise Keepers, a Christian men's movement founded in 1990 by Bill McCartney, a former Catholic, who was then head football coach at the University of Colorado.[16] The movement gathers men for mass rallies which combine Evangelical exhortations, personal sharing, and public prayer. At the end of a rally those who wish to become part of Promise Keepers are asked to make seven commitments: to honor the teaching of Jesus through worship, prayer, and obedience to his Word; pursue vital relationships with other men who as brothers will help each keep his promises; practice spiritual, ethical, and moral purity; build strong marriages and families; support their local church and pastor; reach beyond denominational and racial boundaries; and put into practice the Great Commandment (Mk 12:30–31) and the Great Commission (Mt 28:19–20).

Promise Keepers began as an Evangelical movement but Catholic men are becoming involved in it, bringing its spirit back to their own parishes. In Southern California a similar group has been established called Men of Promise/Catholic Men's Fellowship. Promise Keepers is not without its critics. The movement has been unwilling to include Catholic men in its leadership and has drawn criticism from some women for its emphasis on traditional male family roles. But the fact that it does not proselytize and is supportive of local congregations is winning the movement Catholic support.

## Evangelization and Development

Another significant development is the growing recognition in both traditions of the inseparability of evangelization and action on behalf of justice. In some circles within the Evangelical community, this recognition is bringing about a call for cooperation with the Catholic Church precisely as church. This is particularly true of World Vision International, probably the most effective Evangelical relief agency.

World Vision describes itself as an international partnership of Christians whose mission is to work with the poor and oppressed "to promote human transformation, seek justice and bear witness to the good news of the Kingdom of God."[17] There have been tensions between World Vision and the Catholic Church in the past, as both sides admit. Though it presents itself as a humanitarian service, Catholics engaged in development and relief work have sometimes experienced World Vision as a primarily Evangelical organization using its relief funds for the purpose of proselytizing, and many object to its promotional practices. A number of years ago Catholic relief officials refused to work with World Vision in Ethiopia, though they cooperated with the Lutherans and the Orthodox. In 1990, Trocaire—the Irish Catholic Agency for Development Aid to Third World countries—was sued by World Vision of Ireland for libel. Trocaire's director had accused World Vision of proselytizing with the money they collected in Ireland, and had the support of a number of Catholic Church people from the Philippines. The suit was settled out of court.

However World Vision has been undergoing an internal transformation with important ecumenical implications. From being an Evangelical relief organization with a strongly fundamentalist missionary interest, it increasingly sees itself as a Christian agency committed to relief, sustainable development, and Christian witness at the service of the universal Church. This shift is due partly to the fact that World Vision recognizes that it has a number of Catholics on its staff and among its supporters. And partly it reflects a new appreciation of the Catholic Church's emphasis on evangelization and development. An internal report entitled "The Catholic Church in Mission: Evolution of the Church's Teaching on Development and Evangelization," written by Eugene Daniels, then Senior Advisor on Church Relations for World Vision International, was prepared as part of the "process of reflecting on the meaning and implications of inclusiveness in church relationships, particularly as it relates to the Roman Catholic Church."

Daniels traces the development of Catholic social teaching from the time of Leo XIII through Vatican II and subsequent papal teaching. Particularly important for Daniels and World Vision is Pope Paul VI's insistence in *Evangelium nuntiandi* on the "specifically religious finality of evangelization" (EN 32) and the "profound" link he sees between evangelization and liberation/development (EN 31) as well as Pope John Paul II's firm affirmation of the continuing importance of the Church's evangelical mission in *Redemptoris missio*. In his Preface, Daniels acknowledges Catholic concerns that "(1) World Vision encouraged proselytism through its project relationships, and (2) fostered paternalism through its sponsorship of children." But his conclusion is both hopeful and challenging. He notes "the broad area of convergence between Catholic teaching and a philosophy of ministry embraced by a number of Evangelical developmental agencies," a concern for development as part of evangelization on the part of both bodies, and the need for "a positive response from Evangelicals" to the Catholic affirmation of the importance of ecumenical cooperation in responding to the unprecedented human needs facing the universal Church.

Daniels's report is a part of a transformation taking place within World Vision which represents a rediscovery of ecclesiology.[18] A policy statement on relationships with Christian churches (fifth draft, November 20, 1995), calls on its members to "respond constructively to opportunities for joint participation in ministries that promote human transformation, seek justice and bear witness to Jesus Christ," reject proselytism, and "affirm and promote unity in the Body of Christ." It also challenges them "to aspire to changing patterns of ministry and the building of relations with all expressions of Christ's church." And there is evidence that World Vision is taking practical steps toward this kind of ecumenical cooperation. Recently, its work in the Philippines was reconstituted under a national board, the World Vision Development Foundation, which has responsibility for strategic oversight of its program there. Among its members is Deogracias Iniguez, the Catholic bishop of Iba (Zambeles); he serves as vice-chair of the board and represented it at one of the recent triennial meetings of the World Vision International Council. Daniels himself has worked to broaden contact and cooperation with the Catholic Church in the Philippines, Indonesia, and Honduras.

## Evangelicals and Catholics Together

Another new relationship is represented by "Evangelicals and Catholics Together" (ECT), a loose-knit group of scholars organized by Richard John Neuhaus, a convert to the Catholic Church and editor of the journal *First Things,* and Charles Colson, former White House counsel, now deeply involved in prison ministry. ECT's first effort was the unofficial statement "Evangelicals and Catholics Together: The Christian Mission in the Third Millennium," signed by twenty Catholic and twenty Evangelical scholars after an eighteen-month consultation.[19] Though theologically quite sophisticated, it tends to focus on those moral and social concerns shared by Catholic neo-conservatives and the religious right, among them opposition to abortion, euthanasia, pornography, and the idea that in areas of marriage, parenthood, and family, tolerance "requires the promotion of moral equivalence between the normative and the deviant." The statement supports the transmission of "our cultural heritage" and parental choice in public education, "a vibrant market economy" as part of a free society, and a renewed appreciation of western culture.

Even more significant was the 1997 statement, "The Gift of Salvation," signed by sixteen Roman Catholic theologians and nineteen leading Evangelicals. Among the latter were theologians Thomas Oden, J. I. Packer, and Timothy George; seminary presidents Richard Mouw (Fuller) and Kent Hill (Eastern Nazarene); as well as Mark Noll, Bill Bright of Campus Crusade for Christ, and Robert Seiple of World Vision. The statement was cautious, affirming that the signatories "rejoice in the unity we have discovered and are confident of the fundamental truths about the gift of salvation we have affirmed," while they acknowledge that "there are necessarily interrelated questions that require further and urgent exploration."[20]

But from the beginning, some have objected to this attempt to acknowledge a common Christian mission with Catholics. The 1994 statement drew considerable criticism from conservative Evangelicals for its openness to Catholics, and two Southern Baptist signers had subsequently to withdraw their names because of fears that they might be seen as speaking for the Southern Baptist Convention. Some Catholics criticized it for its conservative social and political agenda.[21] There was even more Evangelical criticism of the 1997 statement. The chairman of the Alliance of Confessing Evangelicals (AEC) said the statement "really sells out the Reformation."[22] Several leading Southern Baptists, including Phil Roberts, director of Interfaith Witness for the Southern Baptist Convention, and Mark Coppenger, then president of Midwestern Baptist Seminary in Kansas City, Missouri, disagreed with its claim at reaching a common understanding of the doctrine of salvation.[23] Nevertheless, the statement has had the effect of requiring those in both traditions to rethink how they perceive the other.

## Evangelicals and Hispanic Catholics

Evangelical Christianity's most serious challenge to Catholicism is in regard to Hispanic Catholics. Allan Figueroa Deck cites a number of studies which show that the Pentecostal movement is the most rapidly growing expression of Christianity today, and that in both Latin America and the United States, Evangelical and Pentecostal groups are gathering significant numbers of Hispanic Catholics into their churches.[24]

Rather than simply criticizing these Evangelical/Pentecostal Christians for proselytizing or "sheep stealing," Deck suggests a number of reasons for their success. Both Hispanic Catholicism and Evangelical Christianity are premodern. Hispanic Catholicism is a popular Catholicism; it "is fundamentally a system of symbols with an exceedingly underdeveloped formal doctrine or theology."[25] Communicated orally within the family, it is "almost totally" lacking rational articulation. Deck sees an "unanalyzed affinity" between this popular Catholicism—with its "concern for an immediate experience of God, a strong orientation toward the transcendent, an implicit belief in miracles, a practical orientation towards healing, and a tendency to personalize or individualize one's relationship with the divine"—and Evangelical/Pentecostal Christianity. Furthermore, Hispanic Catholics are particularly attracted to the emphasis on personal conversion and the smaller, more affective assemblies they find among Evangelical/Pentecostal Christians.[26]

The traditional divisions between Catholics and Christians from Evangelical and Pentecostal churches are particularly painful for Hispanics. Conversion from one tradition to another usually causes painful splits in their families, and there is often pressure brought to bear on Catholic members to leave their "false church." Recently Bishop Ricardo Ramirez of Las Cruces, New Mexico has called for a new emphasis on ecumenism among Hispanic Christians.[27] He notes that there have been offenses on both sides, including an historical unwillingness to welcome Protestants on the part of Latin American Catholicism that has left deep wounds, and he lists numerous contemporary examples of an unwillingness of the two traditions to recognize and respect each other. Nor has ecumenism been a priority for either side: "What is causing Christian dissension at the grass-roots level is the fact that Protestant and Roman Catholic leaders are never seen together, either praying, talking or working in united ministry. If the people see that it is all right to mix with one another, then they might follow our example."[28]

There have been some encouraging signs of a new attitude on the level of scholarship and pastoral formation. The Academy of Catholic Hispanic Theologians (ACHTUS) in the United States meets regularly with Hispanic theologians from other churches and sponsors the *Journal of Hispanic/Latino Theology*. Particularly effective has been the Hispanic Summer Program, supported by the Fund for Theological Education with an initial grant from the Pew Foundation. The program as of 1996 involves some fifteen Protestant and Catholic seminaries and theological centers; it brings together students from both traditions for two weeks of intensive courses, discussions, and worship experiences, mostly in Spanish. Of the seven sessions held so far, five were hosted by Protestant seminaries, two by Catholic schools of theology, and the faculty has included professors from both traditions. United Methodist Justo Gonzalez, director of the program, hopes to expand it to include from fifteen to twenty-five seminaries.

◆◆     CONCLUSION     ◆◆

The dialogues between the Catholic Church and representatives of Evangelical and Pentecostal communities are important. Unfortunately similar representative groups from these communities have not been willing to enter into dialogue with the National Conference of Catholic Bishops in the United States, though there is a Catholic/Southern Baptist Conversation. There remain significant theological differences on questions such as the authority of Scripture, the nature of the Church and its relation to the Gospel, whether it is a visible or invisible communion, a local or universal fellowship, the meaning of baptism and the Eucharist, the requirements of an apostolic ministry, and the veneration of Mary and the saints.

Misunderstandings and tensions between the two traditions remain strong.[29] A booklet recently published by the Southern Baptist Convention entitled *Sharing Our Faith with Roman Catholic Friends* still mistakenly asserts that Mary as "mediatrix" is a dogma of the Church and that Catholics believe that Christ is "sacrificed at the celebration of the Mass."[30] The Neuhaus/Colson initiative, Evangelicals and Catholics Together, has drawn considerable criticism from conservative Evangelicals and some Catholics, as we have seen.

But there are also significant signs of a new and vital relationship emerging from the grass roots. Catholics and Evangelicals share far more than a mutual interest in right to life and family values. Both remain strongly committed to the church's evangelical mission. Both are committed to the central doctrines of the Trinity, the Incarnation, the atoning death and bodily Resurrection of Jesus. And both are concerned with a personally appropriated faith, Catholics through their emphasis on spirituality, Evangelicals through their stress on a personal relationship with Jesus.

Catholics could learn a great deal about what Pope John Paul II has called the "new evangelization," calling those no longer involved with the church to a living sense of the faith, from Evangelical Christians.[31] Some Catholics are beginning to take them seriously, calling for a new cooperation and learning from them about the needs of Hispanic Catholics. Evangelicals are showing a new interest in ecumenism. Some are learning to work with Catholics rather than presuming that joining a Protestant community is the only way to live a renewed life of faith. When Pope John Paul II visited New York in October, 1995, there were several Evangelicals among the Christian leaders who met with him. At that gathering, Pat Robertson pledged to work for Christian unity between Catholics and Evangelicals.[32]

In Los Angeles, Catholics and Evangelicals have been meeting together since 1987. Their dialogue, cosponsored by the Archdiocese of Los Angeles and Fuller Theological Seminary in Pasadena, was for years the only one of its kind. Over the years the members have gotten to know each other and have addressed questions which were particularly sensitive, among them evangelization and the Hispanic community, a crucial issue in Southern California. A number of meetings were devoted to an overview of the Evangelical world and to trends in the contemporary Catholic Church. A full year was devoted to Mary and the saints. When misunderstandings have occurred, the committee has provided a forum for addressing them. The Archdiocese welcomed Evangelical youth workers as observers at its 1989 Religious Education Congress, the largest in the country, in Anaheim, and a Catholic dialogue member attended Young Life's Trailwest Lodge meeting in Buena Vista, Colorado. Another fruit of the dialogue was a friendship which developed between a representative of InterVarsity Fellowship and the Archdiocesan Director of Campus Ministries. Catholic campus ministers have often been suspicious of InterVarsity groups, particularly when the latter have sought access to Catholic campuses. The two youth ministers each brought the other to his respective national professional conference where some of these concerns were discussed.[33]

At a recent meeting of our local dialogue, I listened to an Evangelical pastor—a very charismatic Hispanic, educated at Harvard University and Fuller Seminary—talking about members of his congregation who were former Catholics, as were his own parents. One was a grandmother, "very Catholic," her home full of shrines to the saints, but who never went to church. Another had been a member of the very large local Catholic parish, "but not a Christian; she was doing drugs." After her conversion, she wanted to be baptized, but the pastor did not allow her to until later, when her own parents also asked to become members of the church. A third remained active at the same Catholic parish, but came each Wednesday night for the Bible study, finding that his own life in Christ was beginning to deepen. A fourth also remained in her parish, but finding its liturgy cold, came to the Evangelical church for its warmth and fellowship.

What if the pastors of the two churches were to begin their own local dialogue about the needs of their people? What if Catholic parishes or dioceses were to consider forming some of their lay ministers and evangelists in programs like Campus Crusade and Young Life? What if the growing interchange between Hispanic seminarians were to lead to a new interest, by the Evangelical pastors of tomorrow, in liturgical prayer and a sense for the catholicity and universality of the church? What if Catholics and Evangelicals were to admit how much they could learn from each other?

## Notes

1. See George W. Gerner, "Catholics and the 'Religious Right': We Are Being Wooed," *Commonweal* 122 (5 May 1995), 15–20.

2. See for example David Martin, *Tongues of Fire: The Explosion of Protestantism in Latin America* (Oxford: Basil Blackwell, 1990); Allan Figueroa Deck, "The Challenge of Evangelical/Pentecostal Christianity to Hispanic Catholicism," in *Hispanic Catholic Culture in the U.S.: Issues and Concerns*, ed. Jay P. Dolan and Allan Figueroa Deck (Notre Dame: University of Notre Dame Press, 1994), 409–439.

3. Edward L. Cleary, "Report from Santo Domingo—II: John Paul Cries 'Wolf': Misreading the Pentecostals," *Commonweal* (20 November 1992), 7.

4. Eugene L. Stockwell, "Open and Closed," *Christian Century* 112 (March 22–29, 1995) 318; see also "CLAI's Third General Assembly: An Interview With Felipe Adolf," *One World* 202 (January–February 1995), 4–6.

5. Sergio Carranza-Gomez, "Ecumenical Relations in Mexico," *Ecumenical Trends* 24 (July/August 1995), 13.

6. Cecil M. Robeck, Jr., "Pentecostals and Visible Church Unity," *One World* 192 (January–February 1994), 11.

7. See Kilian McDonnell, "The Death of Mythologies: The Classical Pentecostal/Roman Catholic Dialogue," *America* 172 (5 March 1995), 14; also Jerry L. Sandidge, ed. *Roman Catholic/Pentecostal Dialogue (1977–1984): A Study in Developing Ecumenism* (New York: Peter Lang, 1987).

8. Basil Meeking and John Stott, eds. *The Evangelical-Roman Catholic Dialogue on Mission: 1977–1984* (William B. Eerdmans: The Paternoster Press, 1986).

9. Peter Hocken, "Ecumenical Dialogue: The Importance of Dialogue with Evangelicals and Pentecostals," *One in Christ* 30 (1994),

115. Hocken's article gives a much more complete history of efforts at dialogue.

10. Hocken, "Ecumenical Dialogue," 104.

11. Hocken, "Ecumenical Dialogue," 117.

12. See Peter Hocken, "Ecumenical Issues in Evangelization," *One in Christ* 31 (1995), 4.

13. Kalevi Lethinen, "Evidences of New Life in Europe: Problems Associated with European Missions," an unpublished Campus Crusade staff report.

14. Hocken, "Ecumenical Issues," pp. 7–8.

15. *The Church and Young Life: Partners in Ministry*, 51. This report is apparently no longer available.

16. See Edward Gilbreath, "Manhood's Great Awakening," *Christianity Today* (February 6, 1995), 20–28.

17. World Vision International, Mission Statement.

18. Eugene Daniels, "The Catholic Church In Mission: Evolution of the Church's Teaching on Development and Evangelization," World Vision International, April 1993.

19. "Evangelicals and Catholics Together: The Christian Mission in the Third Millennium," *First Things* No. 43 (May 1994), 15–22.

20. "The Gift of Salvation," *First Things* No. 79 (January 1998), 22.

21. For a survey of reactions, see Norman L. Geisler and Ralph E. MacKenzie, *Roman Catholics and Evangelicals: Agreements and Differences* (Grand Rapids, Mich.: Baker Books, 1995), 494–500.

22. Cited in *Christianity Today* (April 27, 1998), 17.

23. *Christianity Today* (January 12, 1998), 61.

24. Deck, "The Challenge of Evangelical/Pentecostal Christianity to Hispanic Catholicism," 410–416.

25. Allan Figueroa Deck, "'A Pox on Both Your Houses': A View of Catholic Conservative-Liberal Polarities from the Hispanic Margin," in *Being Right: Conservative Catholics in America*, ed. Mary Jo Weaver and R. Scott Appleby (Bloomington, Ind.: Indiana University Press, 1995), 96.

26. Deck, "The Challenge of Evangelical/Pentecostal Christianity," 412–422.

27. Ricardo Ramirez, "The Crisis in Ecumenism Among Hispanic Christians," *Origins* 24 (March 23, 1995), 660–667.

28. Ibid., 666.

29. See David Cole, "Current Pentecostal/Ecumenical Tensions," *Ecumenical Trends* 24 (May 1995), 65–80.

30. Daniel R. Sanchez, *Sharing Our Faith with Roman Catholic Friends: Leader's Guide* (Atlanta, Ga.: Home Mission Board, SBC, 1992), 13, 52, 47.

31. See Avery Dulles, "John Paul II and the New Evangelization," *America* 166 (1992), 52–59; 69–72.

32. Cited in *Christianity Today*, (November 13, 1995), 88.

33. See Thomas P. Rausch, "The Los Angeles Catholic/ Evangelical Dialogue," *Ecumenical Trends* 26/6 (1997), 93–95.

# Chapter 3

# Salvation in Early Christian Thought

*Robert Louis Wilken*

*Salvation,* like many other words in the Bible and in Christian speech, does not carry a single meaning. It can designate deliverance from sin and death or reconciliation with God; it can mean being healed from disease or the manifestation of God's love to the nations; it can refer to a present reality as well as a future hope. In places in the Bible salvation is used, like life or light, to designate God as the source of all good: "The Lord is my light and my salvation; whom shall I fear? The Lord is the strength of my life; of whom shall I be afraid?" (Ps 27:1) Of all the words in the Scripture to describe God's gracious action toward human beings—as for example justification, redemption, deliverance, restoration, sanctification—salvation is the most comprehensive. It is the word used by that great company from every nation as it gathers in adoration around the throne of God and the Lamb: "Salvation belongs to our God who sits upon the throne and to the Lamb"(Rv 7:10).

In the writings of the early church fathers the term *salvation* retains this comprehensive sense. It is the one term used to refer to the whole process by which human beings are restored to fellowship with God through the work of Christ and the bestowal of the Holy Spirit. Later theology sometimes distinguished between justification and salvation, but in the church fathers salvation embraces both justification and sanctification. God sent his son into the world not simply to free us from the power of sin, but also to transform us into people made in the image of Christ. In Christ we are not only freed from something, we become something. "You have put off the old nature...and have put on the new nature which is being renewed in knowledge after the image of its creator" (Col 3:10).

The language and the images used by the church fathers to speak of salvation are all biblical, and the most direct way into their thinking is through their interpretation of specific biblical passages. In what follows I will focus on some of these texts, but it should be observed at the outset that early Christian exegesis of individual texts is controlled by an understanding of the Scriptures as a whole. Unlike modern commentators, the church fathers do not focus on passages within the context of a specific book by a single author, but in relation to what is said elsewhere in the Scriptures. Passages from the Gospel of John are interpreted with the help of St. Paul, and verses from the Psalms are understood in relation to texts from the gospels. It is often instructive to look closely at which texts are associated with which other texts, and how the entire biblical history, from creation to final consummation, provides the context for the understanding of particular passages.[1]

## ◆◆    FOR ME TO CLEAVE TO GOD IS GOOD    ◆◆

Among the many passages cited by the church fathers on our topic, let me begin with three: Matthew 22:39 (and parallels), Psalm 73:28, and 1 John 3:2. The first is the familiar words, "You shall

love the Lord your God with all your heart and with all your soul
and with all your mind." The second is an oft-cited passage in
Augustine's writings, in his Latin version, *"mihi adhaerere Deo
bonum est"* ("for me to cleave to God is good"). The third is a text
that underlies the patristic understanding of *theosis* or divinization.
"Beloved, we are God's children now; it does not yet appear what
we shall be, but we know that when he appears we shall be like him,
for we shall see him as he is." All three texts provide the framework
for the following passage from St. Augustine's *City of God:*

> We offer to him, on the altar of the heart, the sacrifice of
> humility and praise, and the flame on the altar is the burning
> fire of love. To see him as he can be seen (1 Jn 3:2) and to
> cleave to him (Ps 73:28), we purify ourselves from every stain
> of sin and evil desire and we consecrate ourselves in his name.
> For he himself is the source of our bliss, he himself is the goal
> of all our striving. By our election of him as our goal—or
> rather by our re-election (for we had lost him by our neglect);
> by our re-election...we direct our course towards him with
> love so that in reaching him we may find our rest, and attain
> our happiness because we have achieved our fulfillment in
> him. For our Good, that Final Good about which the philoso-
> phers dispute, is nothing else but to cleave to him whose spir-
> itual embrace, if one may so express it, fills the intellectual
> soul and makes it fertile with true virtues. We are com-
> manded to love this Good with all our heart, with all our
> soul, with all our strength (Matt 22:39).[2]

The command to love God is seen here less as an injunction,
though it is certainly that, than a goal. The telos, the end toward
which human life is oriented, is God. Patristic thought is resolutely "teleological." Salvation means that our lives are brought
to fulfillment in God who is "himself the source of our bliss
and...the goal of our striving." Using the words of Psalm 73:28,
Augustine says that we will not find rest until we "cleave to God,"
that is, have fellowship with God and share in God's life. Loving
and cleaving were regularly paired in Augustine and other early
Christian writers, for they knew there could be no "cleaving to

God" without love. As one cannot be close to another human being unless there is love, so human beings cannot have fellowship with God without love. This is why, says Gregory of Nyssa, St. Paul said, "love never ends" (1 Cor 13:8). As long as what we long for is not present, hope remains active, "but when that for which we hoped arrives and faith and hope grow quiet the work of love remains....For this reason love has primacy among all virtuous actions as well as among the commandments of the law. If the soul should ever reach this goal [fellowship with God], it will have no need of the others [hope and faith]...as it preserves in itself the impress of divine blessedness."[3]

The passage from 1 John, alluded to in the phrase "to see him as he can be seen," helps fill out the understanding of the goal. Salvation is always defined by reference to God, not by something that God gives independent of himself. Augustine writes: "God is our reward, in God our end, in God the perfection of our happiness, in God the sum of blessed and eternal life."[4] God is not only the giver but the gift. The first letter of John expresses this in two ways. When we reach the final goal we will be "like God," that is, we will possess those qualities that are God-like, being renewed "after the likeness of God in true righteousness and holiness"(Eph 4:24). Second, "we will see him [God] as he is." Augustine explains these words by reference to 1 Corinthians 13:12 that now we see through a glass darkly but "then it will be face to face" and 2 Corinthians 3:18, "with unveiled face beholding the glory of the Lord," and we will be "transformed into the same image from glory to glory as by the Spirit of the Lord."[5] Salvation is the enjoyment of the vision of God.[6]

## God's Righteousness and Our Righteousness

Salvation is always conceived in positive terms, as the possession of something. It is never enough to speak about being freed from something, to be delivered from sin, or to be forgiven. In the words of Athanasius, "Repentance gives no exemption from the consequences of [sinful] nature, but merely looses sins. If, therefore, there had been only sin and not its consequence of corruption, repentance would have been sufficient."⁷ For the fathers salvation meant acquiring something that was lacking, hence becoming something. Using the Pauline language of the "righteousness of God," Augustine writes: "The righteousness of God means not only the quality whereby God himself is righteous, but also the quality that God produces in a man who is justified by him."⁸

Consequently salvation is a gradual process. Again, Augustine:

> This renewal does not happen in one moment of conversion, as the baptismal renewal by the forgiveness of sins happens in a moment, so that not even one tiny sin remains unforgiven. But it is one thing to throw off a fever, another to recover from the weakness which the fever leaves behind it; it is one thing to remove from the body a missile stuck in it, another to heal the wound it made with a complete cure. The first stage of the cure is to remove the cause of the debility, and this is done by pardoning all sins; the second stage is curing the debility itself, and this is done gradually by making steady progress in the renewal of this image. These two stages are pointed out in the psalm where we read, "He is gracious to all your iniquities," which happens in baptism, "and heals all our infirmities" (Ps 103:3) which happens by daily advances while the image is being renewed. About this the apostle speaks quite explicitly when he says, "Even if our outer man is decaying, yet our inner man is being renewed day by day" (2 Cor 4:16). It is being renewed, however, in the knowledge of God (Col 3:10), that is in justice and holiness of truth (Eph 4:24), as the apostle puts it in the passages which I have just been quoting.⁹

One of the most significant discoveries of early Christian thinkers was that "perfection" was not a state at which one arrived, but continuous growth in the knowledge and love of God.¹⁰ The fathers recognized that in the movement toward God there was a place for the human will. Already in the third century Origen of Alexandria had collected those biblical texts that implied it was our responsibility to "walk in the ways of God" (Ps 81:13–14) or "to resist the evil one"(Mt 5:39) as well as those saying it is not in our power to keep the commandments: "I will take away their stony hearts...that they may walk in my statutes"(Ez 11:19–20) or "it is not of him that wills nor of him that runs but of God that has mercy" (Rom 9:16). How to understand our role in God's work of salvation was no less a theological problem in the early church than in later centuries. Yet all early Christian thinkers recognized that the will to pursue the good and the ability to love God were themselves given by God. Even our holy thoughts are a gift to us, says Ambrose: *"Quidquid autem sanctum cogitaveris, hoc Dei munus est, Dei inspiratio, Dei gratia."*[11]

In the writings of the early church the biblical term "righteousness" is always two-dimensional. On the one hand it designates the righteousness that belongs to God alone; on the other hand it refers to something that human beings receive from God, and hence possess, and is properly called *our* righteousness. Gregory the Great expresses this clearly in his commentary on Job 33:26: "He will render to man *his* righteousness" *(Et reddet homini iustitiam suam)*. Gregory comments:

> Righteousness is said to be ours, not because it is ours as if from ourselves but because it becomes ours from divine generosity. As we say in the Lord's Prayer, "Give us this day our daily bread." Notice that we say "our bread" and yet we pray for it to be given to us. It becomes ours when we receive it, yet it is God's because he gives it. Therefore it is God's as a gift; it becomes genuinely ours as we receive it.
>
> In this situation God renders to man his righteousness—not the righteousness that a person has in and of himself, but rather the righteousness that he received as a possession when he was created, and in which he did not persevere when he fell. Therefore God returns to a person that righteousness in which he was created, so that he may cleave *(inhaerere)* freely to God, dread his threatening judgment and no longer heed the alluring promises of the crafty serpent....Since the redeemed person regains, by a divine gift, the righteousness that was lost soon after Creation, he now fights more vigorously against the allurements of crafty persuasion because experience has taught him how obedient he should be to the commandment.[12]

In his interpretation of Job 33:26, Gregory plays with the ambiguity of the term *his* which could refer either to God's righteousness or man's righteousness. The RSV removes the ambiguity: "He recounts to men his salvation." But the Hebrew can be translated, as in Gregory's Latin, "he rendered to man his righteousness." The ambiguity of the "his" allows Gregory to explain that it is possible to say that something is "ours" yet at the same time to acknowledge it as gift from God. When we receive a gift from someone it becomes our possession, but in possessing it we still know that it was something we received, not something that we earned. Paradoxically, the righteousness we possess is "ours," yet it is something that is given to us, a work of "divine generosity."[13]

Gregory also touches briefly on the relation between the return to God and the turning away from God. The righteousness we receive in Christ is always seen in relation to the righteousness that we possessed before the fall. Salvation is a restoration of what has been lost. In the passage from the *City of God,* Augustine makes the same point, that turning to God, in his words "election," is not simply a turning, but a "re-turning," a turning again, a "re-election," because of the fall into sin. Before the fall Adam and Eve were in possession of certain qualities, expressed in the phrase "made in the image of God," and salvation means acquiring these qualities again. According to Athanasius, the goal is to bring "what was corruptible back again to incorruption."[14]

## Made in the Image of God

As can be seen from these observations, Genesis 1:26—"let us make man in our image according to our likeness"—is a foundational text in early Christian understanding of salvation. According to the church fathers, human beings were created with certain God-like characteristics—freedom, reason, understanding, immortality—and they shared in "divine goodness." In the fall the image of God was defaced and man became subject to sin and necessity, what the Greek fathers call corruption and mortality.[15] In places, the church fathers can speak of the consequences of sin in language as vivid as that of the reformers. "Because of the guile of him who sowed in us the weeds of disobedience, our nature no longer preserves the stamp of the divine image; it has been transformed and made ugly by sin....Human nature has become a member of the evil family of the father of sin."[16] However, though the fathers speak realistically about the consequences of sin, they never forget that being made in the "image of God" is also a sign of possibility. "The end is given in the beginning," writes Gregory.[17] You have within you the capacity to "receive" and "know" God because "the one who made you endowed you with this marvelous quality."[18]

Of course any discussion of the restoration or renewal of the image of God leads directly to a consideration of Christ. Many texts from the New Testament are cited in this connection. One passage mentioned often by Augustine is 1 Timothy 2:5: "For there is one God and there is one mediator between God and man." Our evil impulses, writes Augustine, will only be defeated "when they are defeated by the love of God, which none but God himself can give; and he gives it only through the 'mediator between God and men, the man Christ Jesus,' who was made partaker of our mortality to make us 'partakers of his divinity'(2 Pt 1:4)."[19] Another is 2 Corinthians 5:21: "For our sake he made him to be sin who knew no sin, so that in him we might become the righteousness of God." Augustine interprets it as follows: This text is speaking not about the "righteousness by which God is himself righteous, but that by which we are made righteous in him."[20]

But I would like to focus on two passages, Romans 5 and 1 Corinthians 15, and the way early Christian thinkers used the Pauline imagery of the first and second Adam to speak about salvation. I begin with a text from Cyril of Alexandria's *Commentary on the Gospel of John* at John 7:39: "Now this he said about the Spirit, which those who believed in him were to receive...." Cyril writes: "In a plan of surpassing beauty the Creator of the universe decreed that all things would be renewed in Christ. In his design for restoring human nature to its original condition, he gave a promise that he would pour out on it the Holy Spirit along with his other gifts [Cyril is thinking of Joel 2:28, as cited in Acts

2:16–21] for otherwise our nature could not enter once more into the peaceful and secure possession of those gifts."[21]

This passage is instructive for several reasons. First, it highlights the role of the Holy Spirit in the work of salvation. Salvation is always the work of the Holy Trinity, not simply of Christ. Cyril notes that prior to the fall man was incorrupt and without sin because the Spirit of God dwelt in him" (Gn 2:7). But man "turned aside to sin" and when sinning became habitual, the Spirit, who could not dwell in sinful men, was driven away. Hence, if human beings are to be restored to fellowship with God, the Spirit must return. When God decided to "recapitulate all things in Christ" (Eph 1:10), he promised that he would bestow the gift of the Holy Spirit. Only with the return of the Spirit could man overcome the habit of sinning and hold fast to the good. The bestowal of the Spirit is an integral part of salvation.

Second, the coming of the Holy Spirit is dependent on the work of Christ.[22] Cyril of Alexandria noted that when Christ was baptized the evangelist says that the Spirit descended from heaven and "*remained* on him." The Spirit did not remain on the first Adam because he sinned. For this reason God sent his son, a new Adam who was receptive to the indwelling of the Spirit. When the "Word of God became man," writes Cyril, "he received the Spirit from the Father as one of us...that he who knew no sin, might by receiving the Spirit as man, *preserve* it for our nature, and might again implant in us the grace which had left us."[23]

Salvation only becomes possible because there was a new man, the divine Son of God in human flesh. If Christ had been a man like other men, a "mere man" as the fathers put it, Satan would have been as victorious over him as he was over Adam. The one who came to dwell among men as man was himself God, the maker of all things. Athanasius writes: "For if the Son were not truly God we would not have been deified, and if it had not been the divine Word who had become man, mankind would not have been able to enjoy the Father's presence."[24] Cyril echoes Athanasius's thinking:

Just as in Adam Satan conquered the nature of man, so now he was conquered by human nature. For he was truly God and had no sin in him, yet he was man. And just as the sentence of condemnation for transgressions went forth over all mankind through one man, the first Adam, so likewise, also the blessing of justification by Christ is extended to all through one man, the second Adam. Paul is our witness who says: "As one man's trespass led to condemnation for all men, so one man's act of righteousness leads to acquittal and life for all men" (Rom 5:18).[25]

The biblical imagery of the second Adam gave the fathers a way to speak about the *person* of Christ: Christ is unique among men because he is the divine Son of God in human form. "No one could re-create men in the image except the image of the Father; no one could make what was mortal immortal except our Lord Jesus Christ who is life itself."[26] But the Adam imagery also allowed the fathers to highlight Christ's *work*, specifically his death and Resurrection. For the two passages where the Adam imagery appears, Romans 5 and 1 Corinthians 15, lay particular emphasis on Christ's death ("reconciled to God by the death of his Son," Rom 5:10) and Resurrection ("the first man Adam became a living being, the last Adam became a life-giving spirit," 1 Cor 15:45–49).

## ◆◆ CHRIST'S SAVING WORK ◆◆

It was not enough that the divine Son become man, he must also die. "The Word became flesh in order to offer his body as a sacrifice for all and that we by participating in his Spirit might be deified."[27] Salvation could only come about through Christ's death. Athanasius cites Hebrews 2:14–15: "He himself likewise partook of the same nature that through death he might destroy him who has the power of death, that is the devil, and deliver all who through fear of death were subject to lifelong bondage." And he explains it as follows:

Since the debt owed by all men had still to be paid, for all were destined to die...therefore after giving proof of his

divinity by his works, he offered the sacrifice for all and gave
the temple of his body to death on behalf of all, in order to
free them from the guilt of the ancient transgression, and to
show himself superior to death....So the death of all was carried out in the Lord's body and also death and corruption
were destroyed because of the Word who was in it. For there
was need of death, and death on behalf of all had to take
place in order that what was owed by all men might be said.
Thus the Word himself who could not die for he was immortal, took to himself a body which could die in order to offer it
as his own on behalf of all and in order to take upon himself
the suffering for all men.[28]

Christ's sacrificial death is an integral part of his work.[29]

But Christ's greatest work was the Resurrection. For he was
the first human being to overcome the power of death. All other
men died because they were descendants of Adam. Incapable of
breaking the hold of death, when they died they remained dead.
Commenting on John 13:36, "Where I am going you cannot follow me now; but you shall follow afterward," Cyril says that
"Christ's saving passion" was the "first loosing of the power of
death," and it has given the saints courage to meet death. When
Christ rose from the dead "he presented himself to God the Father
as the first fruits of humanity....He opened up for us a new way
which the human race did not know previously...since our natural
life had failed as yet to crush the power of death."[30] Athanasius:
"Man was incapable of accomplishing this, for to die is what it
means to be human. For this reason the Word, being God, was
made flesh, that being put to death in the flesh, he might give life
to all men by his own power."[31]

The imagery of first and second Adam also expressed the solidarity of Christ with all human beings. Just as what happened in
Adam had consequences for the entire human race, so what happened in Christ had significance for all. He is the representative man
acting on behalf of all.[32] His death is our death and his Resurrection
our victory. "If he conquered as God," writes Cyril, "it is of no ben-
efit to us; but if as man, we conquered in Him. For he is to us the
second Adam come from heaven according to the Scriptures."[33]

Even though what Christ did as the second Adam is done for all and all share in his person and work, his work is appropriated by the believer through the gift of the Holy Spirit. Many texts come into play here, for example John 7:39, already mentioned, or Romans 8:15, "You have received the Spirit of sonship crying 'Abba Father.'" Of this Athanasius writes: "Those who receive the Spirit of God's Son and cry Abba Father have received the power to become sons of God. For they could not become sons, being by nature creatures, if they did not receive the Spirit of the one who is son by nature."[34] But I would like to turn from the Greek fathers to St. Augustine and his interpretation of another text on the Holy Spirit and salvation, Romans 5:5: "Hope does not disappoint us, because God's love has been poured into our hearts through the Holy Spirit which has been given to us."

## The Love Poured into Our Hearts

For Augustine, as well as for the Greek fathers, the gift of the Holy Spirit was certain evidence that salvation is the work of God's grace. For the Scriptures explicitly say that the Holy Spirit is "given." In the controversy with Pelagius, Augustine turns again and again to Romans 5 to expound his understanding of salvation. According to Augustine, Pelagius had taught that the "power of the human will can of itself without the help of God either achieve perfect righteousness or advance steadily towards it." For the Pelagians, natural endowments (e.g., the will) and divine commands (e.g., the decalogue) were understood as gifts of divine grace. "They [the Pelagians] say," according to Augustine, "that the reason why it does not happen without divine aid is that God has both created man in possession of a will that chooses freely, and teaches him by the gift of his commandments the right way of life; so that God's help consists in the removal by instruction of man's ignorance, so that he can know what is to be avoided in his actions and what is to be sought...."[35] Hence to rely on the will and the commandments is to depend on divine aid.[36]

Against this view Augustine argued that God not only endows us with a will and instructs us through the law, he also gives us the Holy Spirit.

> Our own assertion, on the contrary, is this: that the human will is divinely assisted to do the right in such manner that, besides man's creation with the endowment of freedom to choose, and besides the teaching by which he is instructed how he ought to live, he receives the Holy Spirit, whereby there arises in his soul the delight in and the love of God the supreme and unchangeless Good. This gift is his here and now, while he walks by faith, not yet by sight; that having this as earnest of God's free bounty, he may be fired in heart to cleave to his creator [Ps 73:28], kindled in mind to come within the shining of the true light; and thus receive from the source of his being the only real well-being. Free choice alone, if the way of truth is hidden, avails for nothing but sin; and when the right action and the true aim has begun to appear clearly, there is still no doing, no devotion, no good life, unless it be also delighted in and loved. And that it may be loved, the love of God is shed abroad in our hearts, not by the free choice whose spring is in ourselves, but through the Holy Spirit which is given us (Rom 5:5).[37]

Augustine interprets the phrase "love of God" in Romans 5:5 to mean our love for God, not God's love for us, the more conventional interpretation.[38] Here is not the place to argue the exegetical issue, though there are grounds within the text for Augustine's interpretation. Romans 5 begins with justification— "...since we are justified by faith we have peace with God through our Lord Jesus Christ" (5:1)—and ends with the "love" that is "poured into our hearts" (5:5). In Augustine's view the text teaches that justification brings about a change in those who believe: through the gift of the Holy Spirit our hearts are set on fire and we become lovers of God. But the love by which we love God and the faith by which we believe in him is God's work within us. Commenting on verse 10 of Psalm 36, that "he extends his mercy to them that know him and his righteousness to them that are of an upright heart," Augustine writes: "He extends his mercy, not because they know him, but in order that they may know him; he extends his righteousness whereby he justifies the ungodly, not because they are upright in heart, but that they may become upright in heart."[39]

Righteousness is not possible without faith, for "faith," says Augustine, is "the beginning of salvation." Through faith in Christ we are able to do the "holy and righteous commands of God." Christ is the "end of righteousness and...everyone who is incorporated in him through the Spirit, and made a member of him, is enabled to work righteousness, because [God] gives the increase from within. Of such works the Lord himself has said that 'without me you can do nothing.'"[40]

If faith is the beginning of salvation, asks Augustine, "is faith in our own power?" Here Augustine addresses the same question posed by Gregory the Great when he discussed the phrase "our righteousness." Augustine realized that in the Scriptures "faith" is presented as "our" action, as an act of the human will, and hence "in our own power." To answer this question he distinguishes between will *(voluntas)* and power *(potestas)*, the latter referring to the ability to do something, the former to the actual willing of something. It is evident that even if one does something under compulsion, that is "unwillingly," it can only be done by willing it. Hence, even though one's act is not done freely, acting requires willing. Similarly believing is an act of the will; it is not possible to believe unless one wills to believe. In this sense faith is in our own power. It is I who do the believing. No one else believes for me.

On the other hand the Scripture says, "What do you have that you have not received?" (1 Cor 4:7). Therefore, says Augustine, "even our believing is a thing that God has granted to us." Faith and love are complementary for "faith works through love" and there would be no "spark" of love in us

> if it were not shed abroad in our hearts through the Holy Spirit which is given to us. For the charity or love of God which is said to be shed abroad in our hearts is not his own love for us but that by which he makes us lovers; like the

righteousness of God by which we are made righteous through his gift, or the salvation of the Lord by which he causes us to be saved, or the faith of Jesus Christ by which he makes us faithful. That is the righteousness of God, which he does not only teach by the commandment of the law, but gives by the bestowal of the Spirit.[41]

## Theosis *or Sharing in God's Life*

As these passages from Augustine also indicate, salvation in the church fathers is understood as the work of the Holy Trinity within us, the Father who sent his only Son, the Son who as man offered himself as a sacrifice for sin and overcame death by his Resurrection, and the Spirit who unites us to Christ and kindles in our hearts love of God. In the words of an Epiphany sermon of Hippolytus of Rome: "The Father of immortality sent his immortal Son and Word into the world; he came to us men to cleanse us with water and the Spirit. To give us a new birth that would make our bodies and souls immortal, he breathed into us the Spirit of life and armed us with incorruptibility. Now if we become immortal, we shall also be divine, and if we become divine after rebirth in baptism through water and the Holy Spirit, we shall also be coheirs with Christ after the resurrection of the dead."[42]

Hippolytus uses the phrase "become divine," and it may be useful to say a few words about the meaning of *theosis* in the early church. The language of deification is used by western writers (e.g., Augustine[43]) but it is more widespread in the East. Athanasius writes: "The Word became man that we might be deified."[44] Or in Irenaeus's formulation: "Out of his boundless love he became what we are that we might become what he is."[45] The biblical basis for *theosis* is 1 John 3:2 which I have already discussed, and 2 Peter 1:4, "Through these great promises...you may escape from the corruption that is in the world because of passion, and become partakers of the divine nature." But several other texts also came into play, notably John 1:12, "...to all who received him...he gave power to become children of God," and Romans 8:15, "You did not receive the spirit of slavery...but you have received the spirit of sonship." The fathers could just as well speak of being "adopted as a child of God" as of being "divinized." Athanasius writes: "He has made us sons of the Father and deified men by himself becoming man.[46] The terms *theopoiesis* (divinization) and *uiopoiesis* (being made sons of God) are complementary.

The theological basis for *theosis* is that human beings are created in the image of God. As I have already indicated, Genesis 1:26 was taken to mean that human beings were bestowed with certain Godlike qualities, such as freedom and reason, and salvation was understood as the recovery of the divine qualities that were lost in the fall. Like "love," *theosis* points to the teleological aspect of salvation, that in Christ we become what we were destined to be from the beginning.

A good example of how *theosis* is drawn from biblical texts other than 2 Peter 1 and 1 John 3 can be seen in Cyril of Alexandria's interpretation of the phrase in John 1:13, "...born not of blood, nor of the will of the flesh, nor of the will of man, but of God." Through Baptism in the name of the Holy Trinity, he writes, we have been joined to Christ and raised to the dignity of children of God. "Therefore we who are regenerated through the Holy Spirit by faith are called begotten of God." As Christ was begotten of God by nature, we are begotten by grace as children. To be begotten of God means that we are "sharers of the divine nature," because by being united with Christ and filled with the Holy Spirit "God now dwells within us and finds a resting place in us," as is said by Paul, citing Leviticus, in 2 Corinthians 6:16: "I will dwell in them and walk in them." For this reason St. Paul calls us "temples of God," and St. John writes: "If a man loves me he will keep my word, and my Father will love him, and we will come to him and make our home with him"(Jn 14:23).[47]

Participation or sharing is one of the primary metaphors for salvation in the early church. Hence the use of the term *theosis*. Salvation is sharing in God's life, delighting in God's presence, being transformed by God's indwelling within us. Salvation is always *from* God and *in* God. Whether one uses the term "adoption," "children of God," "born of God," "temples of God," "the indwelling of God," "like God," or "sharers in the divine nature," all refer to the same reality: God present in us through the work of the one mediator and the gift of the Holy Spirit.

Just as salvation is sharing in God's life, so it is also participation in the life of the church. Salvation, in the thinking of the church fathers, was never an individual matter; it always had a corporate dimension. Two biblical texts that come into play here are Jesus' prayer in John 17, "that they may all be one," and Ephesians 4:2–6, "There is one body and one Spirit." Commenting on John 17:20–21, Cyril of Alexandria writes: "No one can have union with God except through communion with the Holy Spirit who implants in us his own distinctive sanctification...and brings us back to God and his likeness." When Christ offers this prayer, says Cyril, he does not pray for the twelve apostles alone but all who were to receive the "sanctification that comes by faith and that purification that occurs in them through participation in the Spirit." Christ is asking God to create among "those who believe a spiritual unity, a bond of love and concord and peace"(Eph 4:2). He desires that those who believe would be "united with one another through the power of the holy and consubstantial Trinity, so that the whole body of the church may be in fact one." Then Cyril cites Ephesians 2:14–16. By being joined to Christ and sharing in the Holy Spirit we have union with God, "for in Him we are *all* sanctified." Through the Holy Eucharist Christ makes "those who believe in him the same body with himself and with each other." Those who partake of Christ's "holy flesh" are united with him and become "fellow heirs and fellow partakers of the promise in Christ." Although the Spirit dwells in each one "individually," it is nevertheless "one undivided" Spirit who binds together the "separate spirits of each one of us...in his own distinctive unity so that we are all shown forth as one in Him."[48]

◆◆    CONCLUSION    ◆◆

Most of the writers I have cited lived during the great age of the ecumenical councils, and their thinking is formed by the dogmatic statements of these councils, notably the teaching of Nicaea and Constantinople I, that the Son is "of one being with the Father" and the Holy Spirit is "life-giver," and the decree of Chalcedon that Christ is fully God and fully man, "one person in two natures." These teachings guide the fathers in their interpretation of the Scriptures and provide the conceptual scaffolding on which they erect their understanding of salvation. Salvation is a work of the Holy Trinity, initiated by God the Father,[49] accomplished through the death and Resurrection of the Incarnate Son, and completed by the bestowal of the Holy Spirit. Often these teachings are made explicit. Sometimes they are just below the surface, but they are always there undergirding the discussion.

In the patristic period, salvation is always understood in relation to the telos of human life. Besides the texts I have cited, the fathers quote the words of Jesus in the sermon on the mount, "Be perfect as your heavenly father is perfect," or 2 Corinthians 6:14–7:1, "We are the temple of the living God; as God said, 'I will live in them and move among them' [Lev 26:12]....Since we have these promises, beloved, let us cleanse ourselves from every defilement of body and spirit, and make holiness *perfect* in the fear of God," or 1 Peter 1:15, "But as he who called you is holy, *be holy* yourselves...."

Salvation is teleological; it looks toward fellowship with God, hence Augustine's frequent citation of Psalm 73, "...for me to cleave to God is good." Consequently salvation takes place within human beings and brings about a change in us. We *become* righteous. Yet salvation is always God's work. Even the act of loving God and cleaving to him is the work of the Holy Spirit who is "given to us"(Rom 5:5). In Gregory of Nyssa's happy phrase, the love we have for God is a "reciprocating love" *(anerastheisa)*,[50] love in response to God's love for us. And, finally, salvation takes place only within the fellowship of the church through the mediation of the Holy Spirit who dwells in the church.

## Notes

1. For general discussion of salvation in early Christian thought see Basil Studer and Brian Daley, *Soteriologie in der Schrift und Patristik* in *Handbuch der Dogmengeschichte*, ed. M. Schmaus, A. Grillmeier, et al. Band III, 2a (Basel: 1978); Basil Studer, *Trinity and Incarnation* (Collegeville: 1993), passim; J. N. D. Kelly, *Early Christian Doctrines* (New York: 1958), chs.7,13,14; H. E. W. Turner, *The Patristic Doctrine of Redemption* (London: 1952); Gustaf Aulen's deservedly famous essay, *Christus Victor* (New York: 1956), is still worth reading. For survey article with bibliography see Michael Sluss, "Salvation" in *Encyclopedia of Early Christianity*, second edition (New York: Garland Pub. Co., 1997), 2:1022–1025.

2. *De Civitate Dei* 10.3.2.

3. *De anima et resurrectione*, ch. 7, PG 46, 96a.

4. *De spir. et litt.* 39.24. 1 Jn 3:2 is cited a few lines earlier, at 37.22.

5. *De Trinitate* 14.23.

6. Seeing is a metaphor for knowing and the fathers often talk of salvation as "knowing God." The "knowledge of God" delivers man from sin, says Origen. God became man to "implant in us the blessedness that comes from knowing him and to enable us to have friendship with him through Christ...." (*Contra Celsum* 4.6). To know God is to have an intimate relation with God.

7. Athanasius, *de incarnatione* 7.

8. Augustine, *civ. dei* 22.3. Augustine's language is echoed in the decree on justification at the Council of Trent: "This disposition or preparation is followed by justification itself, which is not only a remission of sins but also the sanctification and renewal of the inward man through the voluntary reception of the grace and gifts where an unjust man becomes just (*unde homo ex injusto fit justus....*)") (Sixth session, chapter 7).

9. Augustine, *de trin.* 14.23.

10. On this point, see Jean Daniélou and Herbert Musurillo, *From Glory to Glory. Texts from Gregory of Nyssa's Mystical Writings* (New York: 1961), pp. 51ff.

11. *De Cain et Abel* 1.45; PL 14, 357.

12. *Moralia* 24.7.13.

13. St. Thomas says that "grace" is something that exists in the soul. "It is clear," he writes, "that grace implies something in him who

receives grace." Grace is not something external to human beings, but something in which they participate. Just as light implies that there is light in that which is enlightened, so grace implies something in the soul. "Accordingly when a man is said to have the grace of God, there is signified something bestowed on man by God" (*Summa Theol.* Ia, IIae, q.110, a.1).

14. Athanasius, *de incarnatione* 7.

15. Gregory of Nyssa, *Oratio Catechetica Magna* 5 (ed. Muehlenberg, 17).

16. Gregory of Nyssa, *Contra Eunomium* 3.10 (ed. Jaeger, 2:293).

17. Gregory of Nyssa, *Cant.* 15 (ed. Langerbeck, 461–462).

18. Gregory of Nyssa, *de beatitudinis* 6 (PG 44. 1269d–1272a).

19. *Civ. Dei* 21.16; also *Conf.* 10.43.68. See also Leo the Great, *epist.* 28.3. "In order to pay the debt of our condition, the inviolable nature has been united to the passible, so that, as the appropriate remedy for our ills, one and the same 'Mediator between God and men, the man Christ Jesus,' might from one element be capable of dying, and from the other be incapable."

20. Augustine, *de spiritu et littera* 31.18.

21. Cyril of Alexandria, *Comm. in Joannem* 7:39 (ed. Pusey, 1:692–693).

22. The fathers observed that in the gospels the Holy Spirit is closely associated with Christ's activity. "Christ is born, the Spirit is his forerunner. He is baptized, the Spirit bears witness. He is tempted, the Spirit leads him up. He works miracles, the Spirit accompanies them. He ascends, the Spirit takes his place" (Gregory Nazianzus, *Or.* 31.29).

23. *Comm. in Joannem* 1:32–33 (ed. Pusey, 1:184).

24. Athanasius, *Oratio Contra Arianos* 2.70 (PG 26, 296a).

25. Cyril of Alexandria, *Comm. in Joannem* 19:4 (ed. Pusey, 3:63).

26. Athanasius, *de incarnatione* 20.

27. Athanasius, *de decretis* 14 (PG 25, 448c–d).

28. Athanasius, *de incarnatione* 20. Some of the church fathers developed the idea that Christ's death was a "ransom" paid to the devil (*Or.cat.mag.* 20–26). But this interpretation was criticized by others, notably Gregory Nazianzus, *Or.* 45.22. For a brief discussion, see Kelly, pp. 382–384.

29. See also the language of the eucharistic prayers in the ancient liturgies. "We offer to you O Lord this fearful and unbloody sacrifice

(*thusia*) asking that you deal with us not according to our sins...."
(Liturgy of St. James) Text in F.E. Brightman, *Liturgies Eastern and Western* (Oxford: 1896), p. 53.

30. *Comm. in Joannem* 13:36 (ed. Pusey 2:392–393).

31. *Or.Ar.* 1:44 (PG 26,104c).

32. The key text here is of course Eph 1:10, "all things are recapitulated in him...." See Cyril, *Comm. in Sophon.* 3:16–18 (ed. Pusey 2:237). Irenaeus of Lyon was the first to develop the soteriological implications of the recapitulation of all things in Christ (*Adversus Haereses* 3.16.6). For discussion see Gustaf Wingren, *Man and the Incarnation. A Study in the Biblical Theology of Irenaeus* (Phila.: 1959).

33. Cyril, *Comm. in Joannem* 16:33 (ed. Pusey 2:657).

34. *Or.Ar.* 2.59 (PG 26, 275a).

35. De *spir. et litt.* 2.4.

36. For discussion of Pelagius's thought, see Robert F. Evans, *Pelagius: Inquiries and Reappraisals* (New York: 1968).

37. De *spir. et litt.* 3.5.

38. See Joseph A. Fitzmeyer, S.J., *Romans: A New Translation with Introduction and Commentary* (New York: 1992), p. 398.

39. De *spir. et litt.* 11.7.

40. De *spir. et litt.* 29.50.

41. De *spir. et litt.* 53.31–56.32.

42. Hippolytus, *Sermon on Epiphany* (PG 10, 854, 858–859, 62).

43. See Augustine, *sermo* 192.1: "*Deos facturus qui homines erant, homo factus est qui Deus erat*" (PL 38, 1012).

44. Athan., *De Incarn.* 54; Gregory Nazianzus, *Or.* 29.19.

45. *Adversus Haereses*, book 5, preface.

46. *Or. Ar.* 1.38; (PG 26, 92b).

47. Cyril, *Comm. in Joannem* 1:13 (ed. Pusey, 1:134–137).

48. Cyril, *Comm. in Joannem* 17:20–21 (ed. Pusey, 2:731, 733, 736).

49. Though salvation is a movement toward God by man, it always begins with God's movement toward us. In response to Celsus who claimed that God could be known by the mind lifting itself up to God, Origen of Alexandria said: "We affirm that human nature is not sufficient in any way to seek for God and to find him...unless it is helped by the God who is the object of the search" (*Contra Celsum* 7.42).

50. Gregory of Nyssa, *Cant.* 13 (ed. Langerbeck, 378, ln. 14).

*Chapter 4*

# Evangelicals, Salvation, and Church History

*Gerald Bray*

What do Evangelicals believe about salvation? For a spiritual movement which outsiders most readily define by its well-known insistence that "you must be born again" (Jn 3:7), this would seem to be an easy question to answer. Whatever his or her background or denominational affiliation may be, an Evangelical is someone who believes that an experience of personal conversion to Christ is the supremely authentic hallmark of a true Christian. This experience may take different forms, but for an Evangelical to recognize it, it must include a prior conviction of sin—which makes individuals aware that they cannot please God by their own actions—repentance, and a changed life. The last of these is extremely important, because in the final analysis, it is a changed life which puts the seal on the conversion experience and validates it. Salvation must be "visible," at least in the sense that its effects must be noticeable. Most Evangelicals would not hesitate to say that if a person does not live a life consonant with what Jesus expects of his followers, then that person is not truly born again, whatever he or she may claim. This aspect of the matter must be carefully borne in mind when we consider what follows.

## ◆◆    EVANGELICALS AND SALVATION    ◆◆

Evangelicals who have had a conversion experience claim to know that they are saved, and feel assured that God's grace, which they see at work in their lives, will in due course guarantee them entrance into the kingdom of heaven. It is this belief, which is known technically as "assurance of salvation," which, even more than the "born-again" experience, is one of the most characteristic traits of Evangelicals, and it is often regarded as a form of arrogant presumption by others (especially by Catholics). How, they might ask, is it possible to know for sure that one is going to heaven? Evangelicals reply that this assurance has nothing to do with their own merits, or lack of them, but is entirely based on the grace of God and his promises to his people. Did not the Apostle Paul say that, for him, to live was Christ and to die was gain? (Phil 1:21). He clearly believed that he would go to heaven when he died, even though he also recognized that he was the chief of sinners and totally unworthy of God's grace. Where the Apostle leads, Evangelicals follow, and claim the same promise for themselves. But—and this cannot be stressed too often—God's grace is now at work in the lives of those who truly believe, changing them and conforming them to God's will *in this life*. So powerful is this emphasis that some extreme forms of Evangelicalism have taken this to the point of claiming that it is possible to achieve perfection this side of eternity, but this would be denied by the majority and cannot be regarded as "orthodox" Evangelical teaching.[1] Even so, however, the emphasis on holy living is a strong one and in Evangelical eyes it goes a long way to counter the charge of presumption. "Handsome is as handsome does," and if there is no evidence of salvation in a person's life, there is no reason to suppose that they are saved either.

We may summarize what we have said so far by saying that although Evangelicals may be deeply divided over many other things, the personal experience of salvation, often described as being "born again," along with the assurance of going to heaven immediately after death, are the characteristics which define them and give them a distinct identity in the Christian world. They are also the things which most perplex Christians of other traditions, including other Protestants. Why is the Evangelical experience of salvation so important to those who have had it that they are often ready to discount other forms of Christianity as inauthentic? Can the Evangelical experience not be found in other Christian traditions, expressed in a different way? And if it can, why do Evangelicals stand apart from the rest of the church? On the other hand, if it cannot, what claim do Evangelicals have to be authentically Christian, especially in a way which implies the exclusion of others? After all, Evangelicals did not exist until about 1740, and it is only quite recently that they have spread beyond the Anglo-Saxon world. How then can they regard all other Christians not only as inferior, but even as irredeemably mistaken in their beliefs?

To make matters worse, it has to be admitted that most Evangelicals have little understanding of their own history and traditions, let alone those of others, and are poorly equipped to answer such questions. The immediate experience is what matters to them, and whether it was enjoyed by others in different parts of the world or many centuries ago is a question which simply does not occur to most of them. Perhaps the fairest way of looking at this is to say that most Evangelicals would see this issue in much the same way as the early Christians saw the problem of the spiritual destiny of the Gentiles before the coming of Christ. Some early Christians thought that pagans were damned, others that they would be judged according to their own lights, and others that there were righteous Gentiles who had as much claim to be regarded as forerunners of the Gospel as the prophets of the Old Testament had. But whatever view they adopted, the early Christians focused their attention on the present and looked toward the future, not the past. Once the day of salvation had arrived, the time for decision-making had come and there was no point speculating about dead ancestors. The important thing was to repent and believe *now*. The rest was a mystery which could be safely left to God.

This is probably the way in which most Evangelicals deal with questions about historical antecedents, although a little reflection (admittedly a rare commodity in most Evangelical circles) would tell them that, unlike the early Christians, they are operating within the context of a historical and largely non-Evangelical Christianity, on which they are much more dependent that they realize. Sometimes in fact, Evangelicals pick and choose a heritage for themselves, which they construct out of the pre-Evangelical Christian past. They look for people and events which appear to correspond to what they believe and claim them as ancestors, conveniently ignoring (or excusing) anything which does not fit their paradigm. Most Evangelicals, for example, would not hesitate to claim Martin Luther (1483–1546) as their spiritual ancestor, and even as their spiritual prototype, although Luther himself would not have recognized their theology and would probably have rejected large parts of it. But Evangelicals are one with Luther on the question of justification by faith, and for them that is all that really matters. His sacramental theology, which retains elements of medieval theology which do not fit into the Evangelical doctrine of grace,[2] is simply overlooked or dismissed as a secondary matter.

The Evangelical debt to John Calvin (1509–1564) is admittedly much greater than the debt to Luther, but even Calvin was not an Evangelical in the modern sense. To take but a simple example, Calvin did not believe that Christians should read the Bible privately, because he was afraid that this would lead to eccentric interpretations of it. Yet not only do modern Evangelicals all do this, they make the private reading and learning of Scripture a fundamental part of their devotional lives. Calvin's views on the subject are simply ignored or dismissed as an eccentricity which he would not hold if he were alive today. It is the eighteenth-century revival in Britain and America which is the true source of the modern Evangelical movement, but even there it is not always easy to say to what extent its heritage is genuinely appreciated by most Evangelicals today. To go no further, the revival was a seedbed of social revolution and a major contributor to the great reforms which took place before about 1850, but nowadays Evangelicals are generally regarded as the backbone of the so-called "religious right."[3]

The Evangelical revival was sparked by the open air preaching of John Wesley (1703–1791) in the years after 1740. Wesley rejected the doctrine of predestination, which was a fundamental tenet of Calvin's theology, because he felt that it was being used by the orthodox establishment of his day as an excuse not to evangelize the masses, who were largely indifferent to religion and untouched by the grace of God in their lives. He believed that everyone had to make a personal decision for Christ in order to experience the grace of salvation, and that it was possible to fall away from that grace by subsequent backsliding. This earned him the label "Arminian,"[4] and there is no doubt that most modern Evangelicals, however much they may profess to believe in the sovereign power of divine grace, have largely accepted Wesley's belief that every person who hears the Gospel is free to accept or to reject it, without reference to what may or may not have been predestined for them. But it should be noted that most of those who press people to make a "decision for Christ" also pray that God will move in their hearts, in order to produce a supernatural work of conversion in them. Far from seeing these two things as contradictory, most Evangelicals regard them as different sides of the same coin, and in their evangelistic activities they generally combine them without difficulty. As the famous Anglican Evangelical, Charles Simeon (1759–1836),[5] is supposed to have said of himself, a typical Evangelical preacher is a Calvinist on his knees but an Arminian in the pulpit!

This eclecticism, however, has not prevented the growth of a more definitely "Calvinist" form of Evangelicalism, which can be traced back to the revival itself in the work of men like George Whitefield (1714–1770) and Jonathan Edwards (1703–1758). The "Calvinist" wing of Evangelicalism has always been its more scholarly and academic branch, and most of what might be called Evangelical theology comes from it. However, it must also be admitted that the "Calvinist" wing is often in the position of being a kind of opposition movement within the broader Evangelical fold, critical of its "Arminian" excesses and generally feared by those most susceptible to the latter. The belief that studying theology will only cool one's ardor for evangelizing the lost is a deep-seated prejudice among many grassroots Evangelicals which no theologian will ever dislodge, and this widespread popular belief usually neutralizes whatever the theologians have to say. From that perspective, Evangelicals who engage in theological dialogue with Roman Catholics (for example) are merely showing another sign of their fundamental lack of evangelistic zeal, and the broader constituency is likely to dismiss them accordingly.

This has to be said, because it is inevitable that any discussion of Evangelical doctrines, and especially the doctrine of salvation, will run the risk of being rejected (or simply ignored) by the majority of Evangelicals, who are unsympathetic to the mindset of those who engage in it, and who prefer to cling, consciously or unconsciously, to the more "Arminian" elements in their heritage. It is no accident that not only have most of those who have been engaged in dialogue with Roman Catholics come from the scholarly "Calvinist" tradition of Evangelicalism, but so too has most of the opposition to this dialogue within the Evangelical tradition. After all, these are the people who are interested in such theological matters, and who can articulate a reasoned Evangelical point of view. But no one should be under any illusion that their views (on either side) are making much of an impact outside these circles, where they are largely disregarded. Christians of other traditions need to understand that when they are in dialogue with Evangelicals, it will almost certainly be with those of the scholarly "Calvinist" tradition,

who may find it almost as difficult to communicate with the majority of the Evangelical constituency as they do.

Having said that, how would "Calvinist" Evangelical theologians defend their doctrine of salvation in the light of the Christian tradition as a whole? All of them, of course, would see it as
the most vital and authentic interpretation of the Bible, and in
particular of the Pauline epistles. "By grace are you saved through
faith and not of yourselves; it is the gift of God" (Eph 2:8) sums it
up perfectly. All Christians would readily assent to the belief that
we are saved by grace through faith, but Evangelicals suspect that
others (and notably Roman Catholics) are less clear than they are
about the meaning of the second part of this verse. To an Evangelical, it means that we can contribute nothing toward our own salvation, that there is no such thing as "cooperating with grace."
Even the desire to believe in the first place is a gift from God, without which no one will respond to the message preached.[6] Of
course, this is an idea which can be found in Augustine (354–430),
and Evangelical theologians claim him as their ancestor in this
respect. But, as with Luther and Calvin, there are other features of
Augustine's thought which do not fit so readily into the modern
Evangelical framework, with the result that many Evangelicals
regard him as having been an "inconsistent" theologian.

This "inconsistency" is particularly visible in Augustine's
understanding of the sacraments, which appears to many Evangelical theologians to readmit "cooperating grace" by the back door.
One has only to read Augustine's account of his conversion (in
book six of his *Confessions*) to see this tension at work. In that
book, Augustine has a personal experience of God, after which he
goes with his friend Alypius to the local church in order to be
"born again" in baptism. An Evangelical can assent to all of this,
apart from the linking of spiritual rebirth to the sacrament; as far
as Evangelical theology is concerned, Augustine was "born again"
at the moment of his conversion, not when he received baptism.
His attitude toward baptism is therefore regarded as inconsistent
with his spiritual experience, though it is not serious enough to

call the latter into question. Evangelicals are quite used to the
notion that "born again" believers can be poor theologians!

It follows from this, however, that Evangelical theology cannot
accept the idea that grace is conferred by the mere administration of
the sacrament, or that a person can be "born again" without a faith
encounter with the living God. It therefore follows that baptism,
however desirable it might be from the standpoint of church order,
is not strictly necessary (Augustine would have gone to heaven after
having met with God, whether he had been baptized or not). This
understanding of baptism as non-essential explains why it is possible for Baptists and paedobaptists[7] to cooperate under the common
Evangelical umbrella in spite of their disagreement over this issue,
and also why some fringe Evangelical groups (e.g., the Salvation
Army) do not see any need to baptize at all. Here there is a real difference between Evangelical and Catholic Christianity which
touches the very heart of their respective understandings of grace.
Why do Evangelicals think this way and how can they justify their
views in the light of Christian tradition?

EVANGELICALS AND THE
◆◆    CHRISTIAN TRADITION    ◆◆

Evangelicals have never really articulated what it is that sets
them apart from pre-Reformation Christianity at the level of basic
principle. When asked about the Reformation, most would probably explain it in terms of the corruption of the church, the revival of
biblical learning, and Martin Luther's (re)discovery of the doctrine
of justification by faith. But important though these things
undoubtedly were, it is doubtful whether there would have been a
permanent schism in the Western Church merely as a result of them.
Modern research has shown that sixteenth-century Catholics were
often very close to the Reformers on issues such as these, and that
there were pietistic movements, such as the *évangéliques* in France,
which were able to stand for those principles without breaking with
Rome. Protestantism would not have survived in the long term if it

did not offer a real alternative to Catholicism, and Evangelicals are convinced that it did (and still does).

Although Evangelicalism as we know it did not emerge until more than two centuries after the beginning of the Reformation, Evangelicals all believe that it represents authentic Reformation spirituality, which to varying degrees has been lost, corrupted, or misunderstood by non-Evangelical Protestants who claim the same Reformation heritage. Indeed, it would probably not be too much to say that Evangelicals by and large see themselves as the faithful remnant in a largely apostate Protestant tradition which is represented by the mainline denominations (Episcopalian, Presbyterian, Methodist—even Baptist), of which they are usually highly critical.

But if Evangelicals can be so negative about other Protestants, how do they interpret older Christian traditions? There is no easy answer to this, but perhaps the easiest way to understand the Evangelical point of view is to say that before the Reformation, theologians thought mainly in terms of the "person" and "nature" of the different members of the Godhead, whereas afterwards they began to think primarily in terms of their "person" and "work." This change did not entail an abandonment of the earlier theological method so much as a refinement and improvement of it. An Evangelical reconstruction of Christian theological development might therefore run as follows.

Ancient people generally thought in terms of "nature" or "substance," and regarded individual examples of any given substance as a "form" which that substance took. For example, "humanity" was a substance, whereas individual people were "forms" or *hypostases* of that substance. The forms might display infinite variety, but none of them could deny the basic characteristics of the substance which ultimately governed them. Christianity was forced to deal with this way of thinking, and in the end the fathers of the church turned it on its head. They had to do this, because in Christ a divine *hypostasis* added a second nature or substance to itself. The incarnate Son of God is one *hypostasis* or person in two natures, which basically means that the person is in control of the natures, not the other way around. This overturned the ancient way of thinking and created a fundamentally new, and distinctively Christian ontology.

However, in this scheme of things the doctrine of salvation, or soteriology, was subsumed in a two-natures Christology, as can be seen in the famous remark of Gregory of Nazianzus that "what has not been assumed has not been healed."[8] Gregory meant that if the Son of God had not become a complete human being, we would not have been completely saved, an argument which in his day was applied to the question of the existence of a human soul in Jesus. It was claimed by Apollinarius that because the human soul was of the same spiritual substance as the divine nature, there was no logical place for such a thing in Christ, because in him the "fullness of God dwelt bodily" (Col 2:9). But if the human soul was the seat of the will, and therefore of sin, which was a willful act of disobedience, Jesus could not have been tempted or have become sin for us on the cross if he had not had one. Therefore, argued Gregory, and the orthodox fathers generally, Jesus needed to have had a human soul in order to be fully human and to be capable of saving our souls.

This incarnational approach to soteriology was standard right through the Middle Ages, as can be seen from Anselm of Canterbury's famous *Cur Deus homo?* When Anselm wanted to explain the meaning of salvation, it was only natural that he should have done so on the basis of Christ's incarnation (why did God become man?). Anselm argued that the incarnate Christ did what no other human being could do, precisely because Christ was sinless. This meant that he had no debt of sin to work off, and instead that he could pay the price for the sins of the whole world. This is what Jesus did on the cross and, when he ascended into heaven, he took this superabundance of saving merit with him. This satisfied the demands of God's justice, and made it possible for sinners to be forgiven, instead of punished for their sins. Christ's superabundant merits are now made available to sinners through the agency of the church, which dispenses the merits of saving grace through the sacraments—rather in the way that an automatic teller machine dispenses the cash laid up in our bank accounts.

That analogy is not chosen at random. Medieval theologians did not hesitate to calculate how much every sin was worth and assign specific amounts of grace accordingly. This grace was dispensed by various forms of penance, each of which remitted a fixed portion of the debt incurred by sin. The excess deficit remaining at a person's death would be worked off in purgatory, although it was always possible to lighten the load by obtaining an indulgence. Indulgences were normally granted for specific acts of piety and were initially personal, though as time went on they could be earned by others and applied to souls in purgatory. They could even be "sold," in the sense that a cash donation could be accepted in lieu of an act of piety, such as a pilgrimage or a crusade.[9] It was against this practice that Luther revolted, and as he thought through the implications of the doctrine of grace, the entire medieval system came crashing down in his mind.

Instead of Anselm's "satisfaction" theory of Christ's atonement, Luther, and the Reformers who followed him, developed a different understanding of the cross. Anselm's views had already been challenged in the Middle Ages by Peter Abelard, who thought of Christ's death more as an example to us of the self-sacrifice which God demands of his people, but although this idea had its attractions in an age of Erasmian humanism, it was a far cry from what the Reformers preached. They did not deny the Anselmian doctrine that Christ paid the price for human sin, but they interpreted this in a different way. They did not believe that Jesus obtained enough merit through his death to pay for every sin ever committed by anybody, so that all anyone had to do was sign on to the church (through baptism) in order to begin benefiting from this heavenly windfall. Instead, they emphasized that *Jesus died for sinners,* not for sins. This meant that all the sins of the sinners for whom Christ died were automatically paid for in advance. In fact, this is how they understood the meaning of predestination. Christ knew those who would believe in him, and he died for them, canceling their sins in the process. This idea cannot easily be squared with the notion that Christ died for the sins of the whole world, although that is also a biblical theme.

The two ideas are usually reconciled by saying that although there is no sin too great for Christ's shed blood to be an adequate sacrifice for it, in actual fact Christ died only for the "elect." In other words, as far as *sins* are concerned, Christ's blood is more powerful than anything which man can do against God's will, and therefore it is possible to say that Christ died for the sins of the whole world. To say anything else would amount to a denial of God's sovereignty over his creation. But in the context of predestination, Christ's saving work is not directed to all *sinners*, but only to those who have been chosen (the "elect"). It is not that those who have not been chosen (the "reprobates") have committed sins which are too great for Christ's blood to pardon—their sins may often be far less serious than those of the elect—but Christ's saving power is not applied to them because they have not been chosen to receive salvation.

This doctrine of the atonement is known as "penal substitution" because according to this doctrine Christ took my place on the cross and underwent the punishment for my sins, which I would otherwise be liable for. Because he took my place I have been set free, and my sins are no longer counted against me in the sight of God. But penal substitution also involves *union with Christ,* an aspect of the matter which is often overlooked in popular expositions of it. This means that although it is true that Christ took my place, it is also true that *I have died along with him,* so that the life I live now is a reflection of the new resurrection life which was given to Jesus after his death and descent into hell. Of course, I am not fully resurrected, in the sense that I am still living in the human body which I have inherited from Adam and am therefore still susceptible to sin and all the other ills which afflict the fallen human race. But in my spirit I have been born again by dying and rising with Christ, so that I can legitimately claim to be enjoying what the New Testament calls the "first fruits" of eternal life. Obviously, if that is true, then there is nothing to stop me from going to heaven, which is what I believe will happen as soon as my earthly body dies. Jesus' words to the penitent thief on the cross—"Today you will be with me in paradise" (Lk 23:43)—have a special meaning to Evangelicals, who see themselves as being in the same spiritual position as that of the thief.

With regard to Anselm's satisfaction theory of the atonement, most Evangelicals would say that the Protestant doctrine of penal substitution is a refinement and an improvement of it—not a repudiation of its essential teaching. The main difference is that the focus has shifted from the sin to the sinner or, in other words, from the "nature" or "substance" to the "person." Christ did not die for things (sins) but for people (sinners), and this is the essence of Evangelical preaching. Penal substitution, the doctrine of the great Reformers, is fundamental to Evangelical soteriology and a major source of conflict between them and more recent ("liberal") varieties of Protestantism, which tend to regard the Evangelical position as "immoral," either because it supposedly portrays an angry God taking out his wrath on his innocent Son, or because it restricts salvation to the elect, or both. In reaction to this, they tend to be universalists[10] and to think of Christ's death in primarily Abelardian terms. Evangelicals reject the charge of immorality, of course, and point to the biblical evidence, which speaks of election from Abraham onwards, and explains Christ's sacrifice in Old Testament terms (notably in the Epistle to the Hebrews). In fact, for many Evangelicals, the differences between them and modernist Protestants are far deeper and more serious than the traditional differences between Protestantism and Catholicism—a realization which has made dialogue with Catholics more attractive than it might otherwise have seemed.

The doctrine of penal substitution ensured that, from the sixteenth century onwards, soteriology (the work of Christ) would no longer be explained primarily in incarnational terms, although the reality and the necessity of Christ's incarnation were never denied. The new emphasis focused instead on Christ's work which, in line with the rediscovery of the Bible which accompanied the Reformation, could only be understood in the context of the fulfillment of God's covenant with his people Israel. According to this way of thinking, Christ was the true high priest who also became the perfect victim, making the final and complete sacrifice for our sins. In such a framework, the medieval doctrine of transubstantiation had no logical place and was rejected accordingly. Christ's sacrifice was a once-for-all historical event which a believer could only appropriate by faith, not by consuming a substance which had supposedly been changed into the body and blood of Christ by supernatural means. The Reformed understanding of Christ's work did not remove the need for the sacraments, but gave them a new meaning in a largely different context. This meaning was relatively slow to emerge, and was the subject of controversy in the early days of the Reformation. Different schools of thought came into existence, claiming to derive from Luther, Zwingli,[11] or the Anabaptists. Each of these continues to exist, but Evangelicals generally see themselves as descending from the position adopted by Martin Bucer (1491–1551)[12] and taken over by John Calvin. In Calvinist thinking, the sacraments are visible representations of the Gospel which cannot be understood or appropriated apart from the preaching of the Word, because they have no meaning apart from a faith which is willingly received. This means, among other things, that there are only two sacraments—baptism and the Eucharist—because only they are directly connected with and derived from the preaching of the Gospel.

Baptism is a form of proclamation, though it must be admitted that there is a division among Evangelicals as to what exactly it proclaims. Traditional Calvinists believe that it is a covenant declaration of God's saving power which may properly be offered to the infant children of believers as members of the covenant. Some would go further and say that this means that all those who are baptized are inheritors of the covenant promises and will eventually be saved, whether they show any signs of sanctification in their personal lives or not. Evangelicals sharply dissent from that view, claiming that infant baptism can only be validated by conversion in later life, without which it is meaningless. Baptistic Evangelicals go further and delay baptism until there is some evidence of conversion, with the result that the sacrament is really a testimony to a faith already openly professed.[13]

In traditional Calvinistic Protestantism, the Eucharist was also an evangelistic sacrament calling for personal commitment to the broken body and shed blood of Christ. For many centuries it was the custom to celebrate the Eucharist fairly rarely, but to precede it with a time of preparation which corresponds to what today would be called a parish mission, or even a "revival." In the eighteenth century however, Evangelicals more or less broke with that tradition by evangelizing *outside* both the Eucharist and the church. Even today, Evangelical conversions happen more often than not in non-ecclesial settings, so that for many Evangelicals the church is not particularly central to their spiritual lives. They get their main spiritual fellowship from parachurch organizations of various kinds, perhaps from camps or meetings run on an inter- or non-denominational basis, or from smaller groups formed *within* the body of the local congregation. So common is this tendency that it is often the case that the Eucharist is celebrated in and by these groups with little or no reference to the wider church. Naturally, this also has a considerable impact on the Evangelical understanding of (the) ministry, since in a non-ecclesial setting the eucharistic celebrant need not necessarily be ordained in *any* church!

◆◆    EVANGELICALS AND ECUMENISM    ◆◆

This aspect of the Evangelical movement needs to be understood since, although its more responsible representatives always stress the importance of belonging to a church congregation, and although there are some Evangelicals who feel quite strong denominational attachments, church membership is not the criterion by which acceptance or non-acceptance is decided in the Evangelical world. In a very real sense, Evangelicalism has always been a parachurch phenomenon. John Wesley, for example, was an Anglican, but he developed a network of cell groups which eventually became a separate denomination—Methodism. Wesley himself resisted this tendency, but saw nothing wrong in forming cell groups as distinct entities within the officially established church. He was prepared to ignore the bishops when they tried to restrict his preaching, and in later life he ordained his own ministers when the church establishment refused to do so. Thus, in spite of his professed loyalty to the Church of England, Wesley actually functioned independently of it, and much the same can be said of many Evangelicals today.

In one sense, this makes them highly ecumenical—far more so than any other group of Christians. Unencumbered by notions like the "validity" of orders or the "efficacy" of the sacraments, Evangelicals are free to go wherever their spiritual antennae may lead them, and it is only in exceptional circumstances that denominational affiliations will get in the way of fellowship among convinced Evangelical believers.[14] Interestingly, this flexibility has also made some of them (at least) more open to Roman Catholics than might be imagined. It is true that there are some Evangelicals who are so anti-Catholic that they cannot accept that any Catholic person can be a born-again Christian, but such people are few and their position goes against the non-ecclesial logic of Evangelicalism.

Whatever they might think of Catholicism as a structure of beliefs, or of the Catholic Church as an organization, it is hard for consistent Evangelicals to deny the possibility that the Holy Spirit may be actively at work in Catholics *as individuals,* or that (rather like Augustine) they may be saved in spite of the system. There are even some post-Reformation Catholics who have been adopted as Evangelical saints, like the famous Mme Guyon, who caused such a sensation at the court of Louis XIV in the 1690s. Mme Guyon preached and practiced a personal spirituality which proved very attractive to a number of people at Versailles and received the support of Bishop Fénelon, but she was attacked (and eventually silenced) by Bossuet, and those who thought like him. Of course, the fact that Mme Guyon suffered a kind of "persecution" at the hands of the church authorities has done nothing but enhance her reputation among Evangelicals, who can fully sympathize with her on that point.[15]

The case of Mme Guyon is a reminder that it is rather pointless to ask what Evangelicals think about the spiritual state of Roman Catholics in general. They look at Catholics (as at everyone else) as individuals, and make up their minds accordingly. Of course, they will usually try to persuade converted Catholics to leave the Catholic Church and join an Evangelical congregation somewhere, but this is so that they can be properly fed spiritually, not (usually) because they are just bigoted Protestants. They would say exactly the same thing to a Methodist, a Presbyterian, or a Baptist who was attending the wrong church—"wrong" being defined as not having an Evangelical ministry. Some Evangelicals would not exclude the possibility that there may be evangelical Catholic priests somewhere who preach and teach the Evangelical faith,[16] but they are skeptical about the long-term viability of such a ministry. They see such evangelical priests as rebels against the Catholic system, which will eventually step in to restrain them and put an end to their activities, and therefore they generally feel that it is wiser for converts to leave the Catholic Church before they come under attack and are pressured to abjure their newfound beliefs.

It should also be said that the nature of Evangelical ecumenism makes it very difficult for Evangelicals to join in the modern ecumenical movement, because the latter is church-based in a way that Evangelicals are not. Evangelicals who belong to mainline Protestant churches are involved in ecumenical discussions whether they choose to be or not, but this does not make them any more open to non-Evangelical Protestants of other denominations. After all, such Evangelicals are entirely accustomed to living side by side in spiritual tension with other members of their own churches who do not share (and who often openly oppose) their theological outlook, so it makes little difference to them if they are officially in dialogue with other denominations which have the same kind of internal division. A reunion between the Roman Catholic Church and the Anglican Communion, on the other hand, would not affect Evangelicals very much, because the hardline Anglican Evangelicals would leave the church for more congenial denominations and the rest would carry on much as before—paying lip service to the official organization but going their own way in practice.

This situation is not an encouraging one for those who want to further dialogue between Evangelicals and other Christians, but the situation is not as hopeless as it might appear. Evangelicals need to develop a coherent understanding of church history (and of Christian divisions) which they can articulate to others. In doing so, they will inevitably have to come to terms with different types of Christianity and reexamine where they stand in relation to them. Probably the best way for them to do this is to start with the "person"-"work" schematization and look at how this works out in the historical development of Christian theology. From that perspective, what would emerge might be something rather like the following.

The first great conflict in Christian history concerned the *person of the Father,* and it goes back to the earthly ministry of Jesus. Jesus is recorded in the Gospels as having called God his "Father," a term which upset the Jews of his day because they imagined that in doing this he was claiming to be divine (Jn 5:18). Knowledge of God as the Father of Jesus Christ was the most fundamental difference between Christians and Jews, and the implications of the Christian claim led them to reinterpret the entire history of the Old Testament covenant. This primordial conflict was soon followed by another one, dealing this time with the *work of the Father.* It was the struggle between the nascent Christian church and the movements which we now call "gnostic." The gnostics accepted that the father of Jesus Christ could not be identified with the God of the Old Testament, but they went on to posit a radical distinction between them which was foreign to the teaching of Jesus. In gnostic thinking, the Father was the redeemer-god, whereas Yahweh was the creator-god, an inferior deity who allowed himself to get mixed up with matter, which to the gnostics was essentially evil. Christians fought this by insisting that the Father was both creator and redeemer, uniting these two concepts in one overarching divine plan and excluding all forms of gnostic dualism.

Once that was done, the way was open to the next conflict, which concerned the *person of the Son.* Arius, with whose name this conflict is primarily associated, accepted that the Father was both creator and redeemer, but refused to acknowledge the Son in the same way. According to Arius, the Son was a creature who was sent to do the work of redemption, but who it was improper to regard as God in the fullest sense of the word. In battling Arius, the church was forced to develop its understanding of the Trinity and to work out a two-natures christology which would do justice to both the divinity and the humanity of the Son. This battle was not won without cost, because before it was over the struggle produced schisms in the church which have remained to this day. The non-Chalcedonian churches of the East are one with us in their rejection of Arianism, but not in their formulation of the one person and two natures of Christ. It may well be, as many people today think, that the problem is mainly one of terminology, which can be solved with goodwill on both sides, but the problem is there and is still awaiting resolution. Evangelicals, of course, are fully Chalcedonian in their theology, although many of them have surprisingly good relations with various branches of the non-Chalcedonian churches.[17]

During the Middle Ages, the church moved on to the next stage of theological development, which concerned the *person of the Holy Spirit*. Here the difference centered on the relationship of the Spirit to the other two persons of the Godhead, and the disagreement led to the great schism between the Eastern Orthodox and the Western churches. The former deny that the Spirit proceeds from the Son as well as from the Father, while the latter insist on a double procession, which they have introduced into their version of the so-called Nicene Creed.[18] Despite some serious attempts, the controversy has never been resolved, and the two halves of Christendom remain divided over the issue, with Evangelicals generally being on the Western side.[19]

The next controversy concerned the *work of Christ*, which divided the Western Church at the time of the Reformation along the lines already mentioned. Modern Evangelicals usually assume that Roman Catholics adopt the "Anselmian" position outlined above, and it comes as a surprise to them to discover that many modern Catholic theologians do not do so. As a result, a good deal of the standard anti-Catholic polemic which one can find among Evangelicals is out of date from a Catholic point of view, though it has to be said that modern Catholics have generally moved away from Anselm's theory of satisfaction. Their position tends to be closer to the "exemplary" theory of Abelard, which is similar to that of Protestant liberals but anathema to Evangelicals—a good example of a situation where Evangelicals would prefer traditional Roman Catholics to the modern variety, in spite of the well-known disagreements which they have with their theological position! Perhaps the best place for an Evangelical-Catholic dialogue to begin is with a study of Anselm. Can we agree about what it was that he was saying? And how do we receive it today? Will it turn out that we have both moved on from there, but in different directions? And if so, can we come to a common mind by going back to that source and looking at it afresh?

Finally, there is a controversy about *the work of the Holy Spirit,* which also concerns the Protestant-Catholic divide. Indeed, it is almost possible to say that Protestant-Catholic differences, and especially Evangelical-Catholic differences, can be summed up under this heading. How does the Holy Spirit actually work in the world? Evangelicals believe that God works in and through people, not things. Thus, for example, the word "holy" can only be properly applied to persons (divine as well as human), not to objects or places. Catholics, with their incarnational emphasis, sometimes think that Evangelicals are not merely otherworldly, but world-denying in ways which are unchristian, but this is a misunderstanding. Evangelicals believe that the physical world must be desacralized in order to be used for the purposes for which it was made. To them, such devotional practices as the adoration of the reserved sacrament smack of idolatry. It is simply not possible, in their view, for a piece of bread to be regarded as the body of Christ, whatever words have been said over it by an authorized minister of the church. The real presence of Christ is a spiritual indwelling in the heart of the believer, not a transubstantiation of material objects.

Similarly, for Evangelicals, the church is a spiritual reality which is only partially and imperfectly manifested in human institutions. Existing churches may be more or less faithful to the Word of God—and of course it is our duty to try to ensure that they are as true to that Word as possible—but no visible institution can claim to be *the* church of Christ in a way which excludes others. The true church of Christ embraces all believers, living and dead, and is basically invisible. That church is a permanent, eternal reality, but its earthly manifestations may be (and are) many and varied. Many Evangelicals regard attempts to reunite the visible church rather in the way that a businessman might regard the establishment of a monopoly: competition, however irritating or wasteful it may sometimes be, is better in the long run because it reduces the chances of corruption and keeps people on their evangelistic toes. Catholics may be puzzled by Evangelical "divisiveness," but it does not bother most Evangelicals because they move more or less freely from one denomination to another, and expect to cooperate across ecclesial lines on matters of common interest—particularly evangelism.

## ◆◆    CONCLUSION    ◆◆

Catholics who want to deal with Evangelicals need to ask themselves whether, and to what extent, they can accept the Evangelical understanding of the work of the Holy Spirit. Evangelicals in turn need to appreciate where they fit in the pan-Christian spectrum, and learn how they can integrate insights from Catholicism and other forms of non-Evangelical Christianity without condemning them out of hand—or simply ignoring them, as they have so often done. Perhaps if these fundamental issues are aired on both sides, greater understanding will ensue and a deeper unity may eventually result. Speaking as an Evangelical, I would want to argue that although modern Evangelicalism is a relatively new form of Christianity, nobody should assume that it has no historical roots. Evangelicals have grown out of the Christian past and have been shaped by the decisions which they have taken at different moments in church history. Some of these decisions, especially the earlier ones, are identical with those taken by Catholics, and Evangelicals are at one with them on those matters (in a way which they are not at one with non-Chalcedonians, or with the Eastern Orthodox, for instance).

But since the sixteenth century they have diverged from Catholicism, and have done so because they are convinced that the Catholic Church has failed to take the right historical road. If they are wrong about this, then that will have to be demonstrated, above all by a deeper appeal to the witness of Holy Scripture. That, for Evangelicals, is where the heart of the issue lies, and what governs their preaching and teaching more than anything else. They are prepared to accept that what they believe now may not be the last word before the second coming of Christ, but they believe that they are heading in the right direction for the time being, and that it is not the past but the future which will determine whether or not they are right.

## Notes

1. Most scholars believe that John Wesley came to this position in later life and regarded human perfection as the fruit of a "second blessing," which is distinct from conversion. "Second blessing" teaching has given rise of a number of "holiness" movements, out of which modern Pentecostalism sprang. However, it must be added that perfectionist teaching, although found among these groups, has tended to weaken and disappear over time, as they face the reality of post-conversion sinfulness more realistically.

2. Luther continued to subscribe to an objective understanding of the Eucharist, in which grace accompanied the elements, even if he denied the traditional doctrine of transubstantiation. His view is nowadays referred to as "consubstantiation" and is not accepted by Evangelicals in the Calvinist tradition.

3. In the United States, for example, Evangelicals were at the forefront of the abolitionist movement in the mid-nineteenth century, but more recently they have mostly dragged their feet (or worse) over desegregation and civil rights, and would certainly not be regarded as major advocates of either.

4. After Jacob Arminius (1560–1609), a Dutch theologian and would-be follower of Calvin, whose views were condemned as heterodox by the synod of Dort (1618–1619). Wesley was not consciously a follower of the historical Arminius, whose writings he probably never

read, but both men rejected the uncompromising predestinarian beliefs associated with "Calvinism."

5. He was the rector of Holy Trinity Church, Cambridge, and a major influence in that university which ever since has been an important center for the Evangelical movement.

6. Note that this is one way in which Calvinists differ from Arminians. The latter tend to think that human beings contribute to their salvation by choosing to believe.

7. Those who baptize infants.

8. Ep. 101.

9. On a visit to Rome at Christmas, 1969, I recall being granted a very generous indulgence by Pope Paul VI, along with everyone else in St. Peter's Square. It was, however, free of charge.

10. To the Evangelical mind, universalism—the belief that everyone will be saved—is really just an extreme form of predestination because there is no choice, but this is not usually admitted by the universalists themselves.

11. Huldrych Zwingli (1484–1531), the reformer of Zurich, is usually thought to have believed that sacraments were nothing but symbolic representations (*nuda signa*) of Christ's work, and therefore lacked any saving power in themselves. Modern research has questioned whether Zwingli really thought this, but this is what is generally understood by a "Zwinglian" position today.

12. The reformer of Strasbourg, Bucer taught Calvin during the latter's exile in the city (1538–1541) and remained the dominant theological influence on him. In 1548 Bucer went to England where he became Regius Professor of Divinity at Cambridge and influenced the development of Archbishop Thomas Cranmer's theology in what we now think of as a "Calvinist" direction. It is at least partly because of this that Anglicanism belongs to the Calvinist tradition of Protestantism, not to the Lutheran one.

13. It should be noted that differences over baptism have little to do with the "Calvinist"–"Arminian" divide, which cuts cross them.

14. This happens mainly when differences of belief (e.g., over baptism) happen to coincide with denominational boundaries.

15. For a good account of Mme Guyon from a confessionally neutral standpoint, see P. Hazard, *The European Mind 1680–1715* (London, 1948).

16. Calvin called such people "Nicodemites," after Nicodemus (Jn 3) who remained a Pharisee even after he had met Jesus.

17. This is particularly true in Egypt and Ethiopia where there is a long history of cooperation between non-Chalcedonians and Evangelicals, although of course there has also been friction from time to time.

18. In Latin one word, *Filioque*, was introduced into the Creed, meaning "and (from) the Son." Because of this, *Filioque* has become the usual shorthand for referring to the debate.

19. This is not always apparent however. Evangelical churches in traditionally Orthodox countries seldom get into debate with the Orthodox Church over this issue, and may even be inclined to take the Orthodox side against Rome (in particular).

# Chapter 5

# Church, Ministry, and Sacraments in Catholic-Evangelical Dialogue

*Avery Dulles*

The term *evangelical* does not refer to a single church or denomination, but includes tendencies within a great variety of ecclesial communities such as Anglican, Methodist, Reformed, Baptist and Pentecostal. For purposes of this article, I shall have in view those Evangelicals who have been engaged in the dialogue between the Holy See and the World Evangelical Fellowship (WEF), and those in the United States who have taken part in the movement (ECT) that produced "Evangelicals and Catholics Together"[1] and "The Gift of Salvation."[2]

Evangelicals of this type commonly recognize that ecclesiology has not been the long suit of their tradition and that it requires further attention on their part.[3] The WEF Statement of Faith, they note, "does not contain an article on the church."[4] The Evangelical-Catholic Dialogue on Mission notes that "Evangelicals, because of their emphasis on the value of the individual, have traditionally neglected the doctrine of the Church."[5] But because they accept the New Testament, which has much to say about the Church, and the creeds of the early Church in which the Church formulated its corporate faith, Evangelicals are in a position to engage in meaningful dialogue with Catholics on ecclesiology.

◆◆   DIFFERENCE IN MODELS   ◆◆

Both Catholics and Evangelicals think of the Church in terms of great biblical images such as the Body of Christ. But they explicate these images in distinctive ways. Catholics tend to interpret the Body of Christ on the analogy of a physical organism in which the members receive supernatural life from the Holy Spirit as soul of the Church. Christ, they believe, perpetuates his presence in his Body through the indwelling Spirit. Evangelicals see the Body more in contrast to the Head, as the congregation of believers who are drawn into moral and social fellowship "by faith alone." With some oversimplification one may say that for Catholics the Church as "mother" begets its members and is prior to them, whereas for Evangelicals the members are prior to the Church: after having been personally converted, they come together into assemblies or congregations and by so doing constitute the Church.

In Catholic theology, then, the dominant models are those of sacrament and mystical communion.[6] The Church may be called a sacrament insofar as Christ continues to be really and effectually present in it, making himself visible under a form not his own. The Church contains Christ and actively mediates his grace, bringing the members into a unique mystical communion. Prompted by the Holy Spirit, the members are progressively drawn more deeply into the divine life through worship and contemplation.

For Evangelicals the dominant models of the Church are those of "herald" and "community of disciples." Salvation, they believe, is achieved not so much through sacramental participation as through faith in the word of God. The chief business of the Church is to preach the biblical message of redemption and thereby form the community of disciples. The members of the community rest their hope of salvation on Christ as proclaimed in the gospel. Many Evangelicals are non-sacramentalists in the sense that they regard sacraments not as vehicles of grace but only as visible words and aids to faith. In the WEF response to the Faith and Order Paper on Baptism, Eucharist and Ministry (BEM, adopted at Lima, 1982) one may find a telling indication of this point of view. "On the basis of this work of Christ [dying as our righteous Substitute] the Christian church lives, not as an institution that dispenses salvation, but as a community of those who have been justified by grace and who proclaim salvation."[7]

Evangelicals tend to be suspicious of the Catholic sacramental style of thinking about the Church. They see it as verging on idolatry and as substituting confidence in the Church for the faith that should be directed to Christ alone. Catholics reply that to overlook Christ's mystical presence in the Church, which he has taken as his Body and his Bride, is to minimize his gifts and diminish our access to him. Evangelical piety, as they see it, is admirably Christocentric but insufficiently ecclesial. Even on the basis of Scripture alone, Catholics believe, it should be possible to discover a more positive role for the Church as the place where Christ continues his saving activity.

◆◆    THE FOUR ATTRIBUTES OF THE CHURCH    ◆◆

In the present essay I shall attempt to illustrate the differing ecclesiological perspectives of Catholics and Evangelicals by considering the ways in which they interpret the classic four properties of the Church as set forth in the Nicene-Constantinopolitan Creed.

*Evangelical Perspective*

At a meeting between representatives of the WEF and of the Pontifical Council for Promoting Christian Unity at Tantur (Jerusalem) October 12–19, 1997, the final communiqué stated:

> The attributes of the Church as one, holy, catholic, and apostolic, which we confess with the ancient Creeds, are commonly seen as a fruitful starting point for further study on ecclesiology. Questions were raised about whether these attributes describe an ideal of the Church, or are somehow already present in the existing churches but require greater visible expression.[8]

The four classic attributes of the Church had already been discussed at a meeting of the WEF Theological Commission on "Faith and Hope for the Future" held at London in 1996. A working group studying the theme, "Toward a Vital and Coherent Evangelical Ecclesiology for the 21st Century," based its report on a consideration of "the biblical teaching concerning the church and the classical description of the church universal (one, holy, catholic, apostolic)." Recognizing the importance of the Church in God's plan of salvation, the report warned against the current tendency to emphasize the kingdom of God "to the detriment of the one, holy, catholic and apostolic church."[9]

With regard to unity this group asserted "that all true believers, whatever their racial, cultural, and denominational backgrounds, should rejoice in their common membership of the one family of God and that together they may with confidence experience the joy of a closer and more visible fellowship." God's gift of the Church, it stated, "entails our task to maintain the unity of the Spirit in the bond of peace." It went on to say that there must be unity on the fundamentals of the faith, but that scope must be allowed for legitimate diversity with regard to secondary issues. More research is needed, the authors acknowledged, to determine how the central core of fundamental doctrines is to be distinguished from secondary issues.

Regarding holiness, the group declared that "the Holy Spirit is at work in and through the Church," which "must diligently maintain its Christian moral standards, striving for holiness in the fear of God." It lamented what it called "scandalous moral lapses by Christian leaders and church members uncritically adopting the life style of their society." Calling for repentance for "our past failures," the authors looked confidently to God to renew his Church.

Regarding catholicity the group made no statement beyond what is implied in its treatment of unity and diversity. With a reference to Ephesians 4:13, it declared that the Church is bound "to strive to attain to the full stature of our unity in Christ." It acknowledged that because of geographical and cultural differences, "there is an inevitable tension between the universality and unity of the church and the specificity of the church in its contextual forms."

Finally, with respect to apostolicity, the report called upon the Church to "contend earnestly for the faith once delivered to the saints (Jude 3)" and to display its nature as "the pillar and ground of the truth" (1 Tm 3:15).

Although the WEF study does not deny that the four properties of the Church are in some way visible, it does not present them as visible evidences to mark out the true Church in contrast to spurious pretenders. While confessing that the Church, as God's gift and Christ's work, is a reality that "the forces of hell cannot destroy," it describes the visible manifestation of the four properties as a task rather than as a given. The body of Christ, it says, "becomes visible as Christians assemble in fellowship *(koinonia)* in local congregations and in larger groupings, as these manifestations of the church fulfil their calling and mission in proclamation *(kerygma)*, witness *(martyria)*, worship *(leitourgia)*, celebration of the sacraments and service *(diakonia)*."

## Catholic Perspective

The Catholic reader of this report will find much with which to agree. In acknowledging the importance of the four attributes the WEF went beyond the letter of Scripture and accepted the normative value of a creed dating from the fourth century. But the elements of the creedal affirmation are biblical. The New Testament clearly depicts the Church as a single body in which all the members are in communion with one another and with God through visible bonds and especially through the indwelling of the one Spirit (Eph 4:4–6). The Church is holy because the members are consecrated to God as a "holy nation" (1 Pt 2:9) and are therefore held to a high degree of holiness. The Church is catholic because it transcends every particular class, race, language, and nation (Gal 3:28; Eph 2:11–22; cf. Rev 5:9; 7:9). It is apostolic because it is permanently founded upon Christ and the Twelve to whom he gave authority (1 Cor 3:11; Eph 2:20–22; Rev 21:14).

The four attributes mentioned in the creed are treated briefly from a Catholic point of view in Vatican II's Constitution on the Church (*Lumen gentium* 8). This text does not identify the attributes simply as notes of the Catholic Church, but sees them rather as qualities of the Church of Christ, which "subsists" in the Roman Catholic communion. Thus the Council teaches, as do the Evangelicals, that the total reality of the Church of Christ is more extensive than any denominational communion, even the Roman Catholic. But it also makes the claim that the Church of Christ, with its essential properties, continues to exist indefectibly (albeit imperfectly) in the Roman Catholic communion.[10] Elements of the Church, both visible and invisible, are present in other Christian communities, enabling them to serve as means of grace for their members.[11]

Regarding the visibility of the Church, the teaching of Vatican II does not sharply differ from the WEF statement. According to the Council the Church is both a spiritual communion of grace and a visibly structured institution, but the communion of grace, although invisible, is primary. The institution exists for the sake of the spiritual communion and is obliged to serve that communion.[12]

The four properties, according to Vatican II, are apprehended and confessed in faith rather than verified by simple inspection. Only in the final kingdom will the Church fully measure up to the divine ideal. The actual realization of the Church on the empirical level always leaves something to be desired. The

Council acknowledges that the four qualities are less visible than one might wish because the essential nature of the Church is belied by the failures of its members. Its unity is obscured by Christian divisions; its holiness, by the sinfulness of Christians; and its catholicity, by the failures of the Church to implant itself in ways suited to the many cultures of the world. Its apostolicity, finally, is marred because many Christians, individually and as groups, do not adhere faithfully to the apostolic deposit of faith, sacraments, and ministry.

The WEF statement includes some positive recommendations for remedying the imperfections and deficiencies of the Church. It proposes that the WEF establish a commission on evangelical ecclesiology to conduct intensive studies of the disputed issues based solidly on Scripture and on previous studies by Evangelicals. Such studies are certainly desirable and could suitably be accompanied by comparable studies from the Catholic side.

*Unity*

With regard to unity Evangelicals and Catholics can achieve significant agreements. Believers of both communities, professing a like faith in Christ as divine Lord and Savior, are bound together in a true spiritual fellowship. Their faith does not remain totally invisible, but manifests itself when they gather to hear the word of God in Scripture, to worship, and to pray, and when they go forth on mission to bear witness and proclaim.

The Evangelical emphasis on the *ecclesia congregata* (the "gathered Church") strikes a responsive chord in Catholic ears, because the concept of the Church as *congregatio fidelium* (the "gathering of the faithful") has deep roots in medieval Scholasticism. Evangelicals presumably acknowledge also the role of the Church as *ecclesia congregans,* gathering the faithful in Christ. When they speak of the *ecclesia congregans,* Catholics have in mind the Church's corporate profession of faith, its sacramental worship, and its ministerial structures.[13] The pastors themselves, they believe, must be in "hierarchical communion" with one another and with the Petrine see, as the center of ecclesial unity. Without these formal elements, the Church could hardly be said to be one.

## Holiness

Turning to holiness, Catholics and Evangelicals may take satisfaction in their common affirmation that Christian holiness derives from Christ and is appropriated by faith in him. Catholics, however, are reluctant to say, as do some Evangelicals, that the Church is holy by imputation, a term that to them sounds too extrinsicist. From the Catholic perspective, the Church is intrinsically holy in its formal or constituent elements—the word of God, the sacraments, the ecclesiastical office, and the gifts and graces bestowed by the Holy Spirit, who has been poured forth upon the Church as its life-giving principle. Second, it is holy insofar as its members are irrevocably consecrated to God, most fundamentally by the sacrament of baptism, but also by other sacraments such as confirmation, matrimony, and holy orders. Third, the Church is holy in the fruits of grace that the Spirit produces in the members, who are nevertheless obliged to "complete in their lives the holiness they have received" (LG 40). The Church's holiness does not prevent it from being tarnished by the sinfulness of Christians, individually and in groups. Thus "the Church, embracing sinners in her bosom, is at the same time holy and always in need of being purified, and incessantly pursues the path of penance and renewal" (LG 8).

## Catholicity

With respect to catholicity, Evangelicals and Catholics agree that the Church has a worldwide missionary mandate, and that it must seek to include within its ranks men and women of every race, language, nationality, and social rank. Catholics agree with what Evangelicals say about catholicity, but they wish to say more. With their relatively positive evaluation of the natural order, Catholics speak of adopting, in purified and elevated form, the native qualities and cultural traditions of all peoples so that the whole of humanity, with all its riches, may be recapitulated under Christ the Head (LG 13). Multiplicity, they believe, can contribute to unity insofar as the various elements mutually serve one another, like organs in a single body. This quasi-organic union is given "from above," because it derives from the fullness of God, which is present in bodily form in Christ (Col 2:9). Sustained by the grace of the Holy Spirit, the Church aspires to become "the fullness of him who fills the universe in all its parts" (Eph 1:23).[14]

### Apostolic Faith

In their distinctive ways, both Catholics and Evangelicals affirm the apostolicity of the Church. The typical Evangelical sees it as consisting in the preeminence of the apostles over the Church, and in the Church's corresponding obligation to adhere to the gospel as attested in Holy Scripture. Catholics, however, understand apostolicity as including God's indefectible gift to the Church in the threefold deposit of faith, sacraments, and ministry, each of which merits special reflection.

In their commitment to the apostolic deposit of faith and to the New Testament as an attestation of that faith, these two great Christian groups have an important bond of unity. The Church, they agree, is permanently bound to preserve "the faith which was once for all delivered to the saints" (Jude 3) and to adhere to biblical teaching as the norm for judging sound doctrine and moral practice. They hold alike that the Church, faithful to its divine legacy, remains "the pillar and the bulwark of truth" (1 Tm 3:15).[15] They stand side by side in the battle against modernists of any denomination who would see Christianity as a vague movement that took its origin from Jesus but is free to accommodate to the spirit of any age.

Evangelicals generally avoid a rigid *sola Scriptura* approach that would eliminate the role of Church tradition in clarifying the content of the apostolic deposit. The very fact that Evangelicals accept the Apostles' Creed and that of Nicea-Constantinople (the second of which names the four properties of the Church we have been discussing) illustrates that Evangelicals can admit something analogous to what Catholics call doctrinal development. The creeds and conciliar definitions, according to both groups, vindicate the true meaning of Scripture as against heretical distortions, such as Gnosticism, Arianism, Nestorianism, and the like. Neither Catholics nor Evangelicals entertain doubts about the full divinity of Father, Son, and Holy Spirit or about Jesus Christ as true God and true man. Whatever disagreements there may be on finer points should not obscure the much more significant agreement on the basic teaching concerning the triune God and Christ the incarnate Son.

Catholics have a somewhat different perspective regarding the relationship between Scripture and tradition. The deposit of faith, they hold, first existed in the form of an unwritten tradition of which Scripture itself is a privileged distillation. The tradition, they believe, continues to live on in the Church thanks to the ongoing assistance of the Holy Spirit. Tradition therefore functions as context and a lens for gathering up the whole sense of Scripture. The great creedal and dogmatic affirmations handed down from the past have authority not simply as interpretations of Scripture but as expressions of tradition. Unlike Evangelicals, Catholics do not find it necessary to measure the truth of creeds and dogmas by reference to Scripture, but they agree, of course, that nothing contrary to Scripture can belong to the deposit of faith.

## ◆◆ APOSTOLIC SACRAMENTS ◆◆

With regard to sacraments, the differences are perhaps sharper, but there is room for significant rapprochement. Evangelicals are not, as a group, anti-sacramental. Many of them, conceding that the Church has from the beginning practiced sacramental worship, contend that such practice should continue. According to Donald Carson, the "overwhelming majority" of Evangelicals are happy to reckon sacraments (or "ordinances") as "one of the defining marks of the church." But he notes that "evangelicals do not elevate sacraments/ordinances to the level of *primary* importance."[16] With their concentration on the Word of God, Evangelicals are wary of what they call "sacramentalism." According to the WEF critique of BEM, many Evangelicals avoid the use of the word "sacrament" because it tends to suggest the idea of a sign that is efficacious simply by virtue of the rite itself. This view of sacramental efficacy, which they attribute to Catholics, strikes them as magical.[17]

According to the Catholic view, by contrast, sacraments, no less than Scripture, pertain to the apostolic deposit; they owe their efficacy to the continued presence of Christ who remains with the Church, working through the Holy Spirit. During his earthly ministry Christ conferred his blessings not only by word but also by gestures and other symbolic actions. If he continues to speak through the proclaimed word, why should he not continue to act through sacramental rites? Prima facie, the New Testament seems to say that he does.

Although Catholics do not construct their sacramental theology on the basis of Scripture alone, they hold that Scripture supports their view that sacraments, especially the two great sacraments of baptism and the Eucharist, are constitutive of the Church. These two sacraments are the rites most clearly attested by Scriptures as having been divinely instituted.

*Baptism and Church*

Christians are commanded to baptize by Jesus himself according to Matthew 28:19, which records the "great commission," and Mark 16:16, which adds that "he who believes and is baptized will be saved." Similarly in the Fourth Gospel, Jesus, speaking to Nicodemus, declares that it is necessary to be born of "water and the Holy Spirit" in order to enter the Kingdom of God (Jn 3:5)—a text that most exegetes understand as referring to baptism.

Some Evangelicals, especially those known as "Baptists," do

not see baptism as essential either for salvation or for Church membership. For them it is a kind of seal to verify in a public way the faith already held and professed as a result of personal conversion. A recent document from the Baptist Church Union of Great Britain points out the ecumenical significance of this view of Christian initiation. Baptists, it states, may be seen as difficult partners because, unlike most other Christians, they do not recognize baptism as the fundamental sign of unity among Christians. But the report continues:

> However, as Baptists, our direction of thought is *from* the nature of the church *to* the meaning of baptism: it is because we understand the core of the church community to be committed disciples of Christ...that we understand baptism to be the seal of the Spirit for a believing and obedient disciple. At the same time, this means that we can recognize the realities of church and ministry existing among others, regardless of the mode of baptism they exercise....[18]

To dispel any impression of magic, it is important to note that baptism in the New Testament and in Catholic theology is not a substitute for personal conversion and faith, both of which are necessary. But the rite itself is no mere formality. It is seen as an integral component of the process of conversion and as the door of entry to the Church.

In the apostolic age converts were not considered to be incorporated into the Church until they had been baptized. When Paul writes to believers in churches he had not yet visited, he takes it for granted that they have been baptized (Rom 6:4; Col 2:12). The Book of Acts presents the same picture. Those who by exception received the Spirit in advance were forthwith baptized and thereby brought into the Christian community (Acts 10:44–48). The curious anomaly of the disciples at Ephesus who had received only the baptism of John confirms the rule, because their situation was promptly rectified by the administration of Christian baptism (Acts 19:1–7).

Besides presenting baptism as divinely instituted and as necessary for Christian initiation, the New Testament depicts baptism as a salvific rite, which washes away sin and confers the Holy

Spirit. Thus Peter in his first Pentecost sermon can tell his converts to repent and be baptized so as to receive forgiveness of their sins and the gift of the Holy Spirit (Acts 2:38). Ananias later instructs Paul to "rise, be baptized, and wash away your sins" (Acts 22:16). Many other New Testament texts speak of washing where the reference is almost certainly to baptism (1 Cor 6:11; Eph 5:26; Ti 3:5; Heb 10:22). In the First Letter of Peter we read that just as Noah and his family were saved from the flood by entering the ark, so Christians are saved by entering the Church through the waters of baptism (1 Pt 3:20–21). Paul asserts that by baptism Christians "have put on Christ" (Gal 3:27). He attributes the efficacy of the rite to the Holy Spirit: "By the Spirit we were all baptized into one body, Jews or Greeks, slaves or free" (1 Cor 12:13). Because the Church is one, baptism is likewise one. Administered by the command of God, in the name of the Lord, and by the power of the Spirit, baptism, as the sacrament of the one faith, incorporates its recipients into the one Church (cf. Eph 4:3–5).[19]

There are many disputed questions about baptism which it is not possible to treat in the present context. My intention is simply to affirm that baptism is one of those rites of the Church which by reason of its divine institution and saving efficacy belongs inalienably to the process of Christian initiation. This view of baptism seems to Catholics to be biblically warranted and pertinent to the Church's apostolicity.

## Eucharist and Church

Evangelical Christians differ greatly from one another in their eucharistic theology and practice. For many of them, according to James Packer, "the Lord's Supper…becomes an event of spiritual refreshment through thankful, intentional remembering of Christ's cross and self-offering to him in gratitude for it." So understood, it may be considered a means of grace, conveying or confirming the benefits it signifies, through the active exercise of faith that it evokes.[20] For Catholics, as is well known, the Eucharist is the central act of Christian worship, in which Jesus makes himself really and substantially present as our once-for-all victim and food. If the sacraments build the Church, this is eminently true of the Eucharist, which draws the faithful into Christ's redemptive sacrifice and nourishes them with the food of eternal life.

The biblical evidence concerning the Eucharist is less abundant than for baptism, but nevertheless compelling. The institution of the rite by Jesus is clearly taught in the Synoptic Gospels (Mt 26:26–29; Mk 14:22–25; Lk 22:15–20) as well as by Paul (1 Cor 11:23–25). The Fourth Gospel, in recounting the discourse of Jesus at Capharnaum, brings out the realism of his presence as food and drink (Jn 6:53–59). The rite of the "breaking of the bread" in Acts is generally understood as including the Lord's Supper or even as a *terminus technicus* for that Supper. The sacred meal is, together with the apostles' teaching and fellowship, a constituent note of the Church (Acts 2:42; cf. 2:46; 20:7).

The ecclesial dimension of the Eucharist is manifest in the teaching of Paul. It brings about the unity it symbolizes. "Because there is one bread, we who are many are one body, for we all partake of the one bread" (1 Cor 10:17). The divine institution of this sacrament is attested by the command: "Do this in remembrance of me" (1 Cor 11:25; cf. Lk 22:19). Paul, moreover, affirms a realistic doctrine concerning the presence of Christ in the elements: "The cup of blessing which we bless, is it not a participation in the blood of Christ? The bread which we break, is it not a participation in the body of Christ?" (1 Cor 10:16). To eat and drink without discerning the body is to bring judgment upon oneself (1 Cor 11:29).

From all these texts it seems clear that a Church which did not baptize and celebrate the Lord's Supper would be deficient in apostolicity. It would fall seriously short of fidelity to the Scriptures themselves. Calvinists, Anglicans, and Lutherans, no less than the Catholics and Orthodox, have recognized this. For a promising dialogue on ecclesiology it is important that these two sacraments, at least, be recognized as building blocks of the Church.

## APOSTOLIC MINISTRY

Besides revealed doctrine and sacraments, a third constituent of apostolicity, in the Catholic view, is the apostolic ministry. Here again, there is difference between the typical Evangelical and Catholic positions. The Evangelicals see the Church as being under the authority of the apostles, expressed in Scripture. While fully acknowledging this, Catholics are convinced that the teaching and governing office of the apostles is perpetuated by the hierarchical magisterium, which enjoys the abiding assistance of the Holy Spirit, including its power to authenticate the canon of Scripture and to interpret the inspired text.

In the early Church, as we know it from Scripture, the transmission of the apostolic faith and the government of the community were not left to chance, but were supervised by the apostolic leadership. Jesus himself carefully trained the Twelve, whom he chose to be his witnesses after his death. The Book of Acts shows the way in which the apostolic leadership supervised the teaching and practices of the Christian community in every locality where the gospel was received.

As the Church expanded, the original Twelve shared their authority and the title of "apostle" with others, such as Matthias, Paul, and Barnabas. Paul records that after receiving direct revelations from the risen Christ, he received the "right hand of fellowship" from Peter, James, and John (Gal 2:9). Through visitations and letters, the apostles exercise close oversight over the young churches to prevent any corruption of the gospel. While Paul recognizes other ministries as coming from the Holy Spirit in a charismatic way, he does not hesitate to appeal to his own apostolic authority in order to correct excesses and deviations (1 Cor 9:1–3; 15:8–9; Gal 1:11–16). He insists that his teaching on central truths such as the Eucharist and the Resurrection must be accepted because it is the common doctrine of the apostles, whose testimony is peremptory (1 Cor 11:23; 15:3, 11; 1 Thes 2:6).

Wherever Paul and Barnabas evangelize in Asia Minor, they ordain presbyters to carry on their ministry (Acts 14:23). Figures such as Timothy, Titus, Mark, and Epaphroditus emerge as approved hierarchical leaders. By the early decades of the second century the government of the churches by bishops seems to have become all but universal. The bishops received the fullness of the apostolic ministry in its transmissible aspects, and thus became the principal office-holders in the Church. After the conversion of Constantine, when Christianity became the dominant religion in the Empire, it became necessary and possible for the bishops to make collegial decisions about the orthodoxy of certain doctrines and practices. Certain councils, recognized as speaking for the whole Church, were designated as ecumenical, and their decisions were considered normative and binding on all Christians. The creed of the Council of Nicea, and its variant form later approved by the Council of Constantinople, have been accepted as standards of orthodoxy by nearly all Christians. To call these decisions into question, as some Christians seek to do in our time, is to regress to a more primitive state and fall back into the very confusion that the councils dispelled.

Study of Scripture alone does not yield a complete theory of apostolic succession in the ministry. It does not give clear information about the specific role of bishops as distinct from presbyters and others, nor does it tell us much about succession in the Petrine office. Regarding such matters, we must draw on the resources of tradition. But even from Scripture alone it is possible to conclude that Christ instituted an authoritative apostolic ministry, which was maintained in full force throughout the New Testament period.

The Catholic Church teaches that in making provision for the unity of the episcopate, the Lord gave a primacy of authority to Peter and his successors. Biblical scholars have no difficulty in recognizing the preeminent position of Peter in the apostolic age.[21] The Bible itself does not say anything directly about the Petrine succession, which came to be recognized only gradually, with the passage of centuries. By the time of Cyprian in the third century, the unique relationship between the bishop of Rome and Peter was acknowledged. The rationale behind Petrine primacy was expressed by the First Vatican Council:

In order that the episcopate itself should be one and undivided and that the whole multitude of believers should be held together in the unity of faith and communion by means of a closely united priesthood, he set blessed Peter over the rest of the apostles and instituted in him the permanent principle and visible foundation of this twofold unity. [DS 3051]

The problem of succession in the Petrine office, since it is not explicitly dealt with in the New Testament, will presumably remain an open question between Catholics and those Evangelicals who recognize Scripture alone as the norm of correct doctrine. If the bishops are seen as successors of the apostles, it would seem highly probable that the body of bishops would have a primate, as did the college of the apostles. But for full certitude in the matter it is necessary to look beyond the New Testament, which does not recount the history of Peter's ministry in Rome or the events that followed his death.

◆◆　　CONCLUSION　　◆◆

Following a suggestion of the Tantur meeting of 1997, I have attempted in these pages to see how far the four classical attributes of the Church will bring us in an Evangelical-Catholic rapprochement in ecclesiology. Since both sides affirm the same four attributes, the convergence is significant and encouraging. But because the two sides operate on different ecclesiological models—predominance being given to the herald model and the community of disciples on the Evangelical side and to the sacramental model and mystical communion on the Catholic side—full agreement is elusive. Is the Church's unity the social union of a congregation of believers in the same Lord? Or is it the quasi-organic unity of a body animated by the same Holy Spirit? Is the holiness of the Church that of Christ imputed to the community and held up to it as an ideal? Or is it the holiness of a people made sacred by consecration to the Lord? Is catholicity to be defined simply as the Church's mandate to preach the gospel to all peoples and to be a fellowship transcending all social barriers? Or does it involve, additionally, a participation in the fullness of God and of Christ the Son of God?

The application of the fourth note, apostolicity, has proved especially complex. Catholics and Evangelicals agree that the inspired and canonical Scriptures constitute an abiding norm of apostolicity in Christian doctrine, worship, and morality. This is already a very significant point of unity. But for Catholics apostolicity extends beyond Scripture to tradition, sacraments, and sacred ministry. In the Catholic view, the sacraments of baptism and Eucharist were instituted by Christ as means of grace and salvation. Apostolic succession in the episcopal and Petrine offices, they believe, is a divinely given means without which the apostolic faith cannot be maintained in its purity and fullness.

These differences should not be simply noted in a spirit of passive resignation. In dialogue we must attempt to hear one another and to go beyond what we would have thought in isolation. In this essay and other writings I have tried to express my esteem for the herald model of the Church, which admirably sustains a living faith in the gospel message and a zeal to proclaim that message. I have also supported the model of "community of disciples," which lends itself to a fully Catholic interpretation. While Catholics seek to profit from what Evangelicals have to teach them, they will urge Evangelicals to be more hospitable to the sacramental model and to the concept of mystical communion that normally goes with that model.

I have here contended that Scripture alone, read without prior commitment to a particular denominational position, presents the Church as the Body and Spouse of Christ, animated by his Spirit, who dwells in individual believers and in the Church as a whole, making it into a mysterious communion of grace and love. As a kind of corporate sacrament, the Church is a sign and instrument of Christ's abiding presence with the community and its leaders. The sacramentality of the Church pervades all dimensions of its life, but is especially manifest in baptism, whereby its members are consecrated to the Lord, and in the Eucharist, whereby they enter into the heart of the Paschal mystery. If Evangelical

Christians could accept the measure of sacramentality that is attested by Scripture itself, the present dialogue would be rich in promise. The way would be clear for a discussion whether the post-biblical developments in Catholic faith and order are consonant with the biblical foundations or at odds with them.

## Notes

1. "Evangelicals and Catholics Together: The Christian Mission in the Third Millennium," published in *First Things* No. 43 (May 1994), 15–22.

2. "The Gift of Salvation," published in *First Things* No. 79 (January 1998), 20–23.

3. According to one Evangelical: "It must be frankly admitted that most Evangelicals have devoted much less time to ecclesiology than to, say, bibliology, Bible exposition or the atonement." So writes Donald A. Carson in "Evangelicals, Ecumenism, and the Church" in *Evangelical Affirmations*, ed. Kenneth S. Kantzer and Carl F. H. Henry (Grand Rapids, Mich.: Zondervan, 1990), 347–385, at 354.

4. Paul Schrotenboer, ed., "An Evangelical Response to *Baptism, Eucharist and Ministry*," *Evangelical Review of Theology* 13 (1989), 291–313, at 293. The text of the Statement of Faith (1951) is quoted in David M. Howard, *The Dream That Would Not Die* (Exeter, Eng.: The Paternoster Press, 1986), 31. The Report of Working Group 5 of the WEF conference of 1986 on "Faith and Hope for the Future" proposed that consideration be given to revising the WEF Basis of Faith with the addition of a clearer statement on the Church. See text in *Evangelical Review of Theology* 21 (January 1997), 21–22, at 22.

5. *The Evangelical-Roman Catholic Dialogue on Mission, 1977–1984*, ed. Basil Meeking and John Stott (Grand Rapids, Mich.: Eerdmans, 1986), 65.

6. For a fuller discussion of the Church as sacrament, mystical communion, herald, and community of disciples see Avery Dulles, *Models of the Church*, expanded Image Books ed. (New York: Doubleday, 1987).

7. "Evangelical Response to *Baptism, Eucharist and Ministry*," 303.

8. The Final Communiqué was published in the *Information Service* of the Pontifical Council for Promoting Christian Unity, n. 96 (1997/IV), 137–138.

9. "Report of Working Group 5," 21 and 22.

10. This balance between indefectibility and imperfection is illustrated in the statement of the Decree on Ecumenism on unity: "This unity, we believe, dwells in the Catholic Church as something she can never lose, and we hope that it will continue to increase until the end of time" (UR 4). The same could be said regarding the Church's holiness, catholicity, and apostolicity.

11. Vatican II, Decree on Ecumenism, *Unitatis redintegratio*, 3.

12. *Lumen gentium* 8 draws an analogy of proportionality between the two natures of Christ and the two aspects of the Church. Just as the humanity of Christ serves the divinity, so the visible institution of the Church serves the mystical communion.

13. Vatican II teaches that for full incorporation in the Church it is necessary to accept the full structure and be joined to it "by the bonds of profession of faith, the sacraments, ecclesiastical government and communion" (*Lumen gentium* 14).

14. On the concept of catholicity see Avery Dulles, *The Catholicity of the Church* (Oxford: Clarendon Press, 1985), especially chapter 2, "Catholicity from Above: The Fullness of God in Christ," 30–47.

15. The "Report of Group 5" asserts that "in this age of religious pluralism and relativism" the Church must "clearly display its nature as the pillar and ground of the truth (1 Tm 3:15)," 21.

16. Carson, "Evangelicals, Ecumenism, and the Church," 376.

17. "Evangelical Response to *Baptism, Eucharist and Ministry*," 312–313.

18. "Believing and Being Baptized: Baptism, So-Called Rebaptism and Children in the Church," a discussion document by the Doctrine and Worship Committee of the Baptist Union of Great Britain, 1996; quoted by S. Mark Heim, "Baptismal Recognition and the Baptist Churches," in *Baptism and the Unity of the Church*, ed. Michael Root and Risto Saarinen (Grand Rapids, Mich.: Eerdmans, 1998), 150–163, at 152.

19. The "Evangelical Response to *Baptism, Eucharist and Ministry*" protests that many of the passages cited by the Lima document (and in the preceding paragraphs of this article) do not refer to water-baptism. It accuses BEM of relying "far too heavily on church tradition that cannot be traced back to the New Testament itself" (296). But this

charge raises the question whether non-sacramentalist Evangelicals are not allowing their own particular traditions to influence unduly their reading of the New Testament.

20. James I. Packer, "Crosscurrents among Evangelicals," in *Evangelicals and Catholics Together*, ed. Charles Colson and Richard John Neuhaus (Dallas, Tex.: Word, 1995), 147–174, at 152.

21. For a synthesis of the ecumenical consensus among contemporary exegetes see *Peter in the New Testament*, ed. Raymond E. Brown, Karl P. Donfried, and John Reumann (Minneapolis: Augsburg, and New York: Paulist, 1973).

*Chapter 6*

# Toward an Evangelical Ecclesiology

*Timothy George*

On July 29, 1928, a young evangelical pastor began his sermon on Saint Paul's discourse on the Body of Christ in 1 Corinthians 12 with these words:

> There is a word that, when a Catholic hears it, kindles all his feeling of love and bliss; that stirs all the depths of his religious sensibility, from dread and awe of the Last Judgment to the sweetness of God's presence; and that certainly awakens in him the feeling of home; the feeling that only a child has in relation to its mother, made up of gratitude, reverence, and devoted love; the feeling that overcomes one when, after a long absence, one returns to one's home, the home of one's childhood.

122

> And there is a word that to Protestants has the sound of something infinitely commonplace, more or less indifferent and superfluous, that does not make their heart beat faster; something with which a sense of boredom is so often associated, or which at any rate does not lend wings to our religious feelings—and yet our fate is sealed, if we are unable again to attach a new, or perhaps a very old, meaning to it. Woe to us if that word does not become important to us soon again, does not become important in our lives.
>
> Yes, the word to which I am referring is "Church," the meaning of which we propose to look at today.[1]

These words were spoken by Dietrich Bonhoeffer to a small German-speaking congregation in Barcelona, Spain. They present both a diagnosis and a challenge for evangelicals today who are called upon to set forth a clear, compelling ecclesiology in the light of new conversations and developing relations with their Roman Catholic brothers and sisters.

As an international, transdenominational fellowship of some one-half billion believers around the world, evangelicalism is in its very existence an amazing ecumenical fact. As a theological movement, however, evangelicalism has been slow to develop a distinctive ecclesiology and that for several reasons. First, evangelical scholars have been preoccupied with other theological themes such as biblical revelation, religious epistemology and apologetics. Second, as an activist movement committed to evangelism, missions, and church planting, evangelicalism has not made reflective ecclesiology a high priority. As some might choose to put it, "We are too busy winning people to Christ to engage in something which seems too much like navel-gazing."[2] This objection should not be gainsaid, especially when coupled with the warning by missiologist J. C. Hoekendijk who observed that "in history a keen ecclesiological interest has, almost without exception, been a sign of spiritual decadence."[3] Third, evangelicalism is a fissiparous movement of bewildering diversity made up of congregations, denominations, and parachurch movements whose shared identity is not tied to a particular view of church polity or ministerial orders. Amidst such variety is it even possible to describe one single, or even central, evangelical ecclesiology?

These objections sharpen the discussion, but they must not forestall our pressing forward with the kind of sustained ecclesial reflection called for not only by the present ecumenical moment but, more importantly, by biblical Christianity and Reformation theology which are at the wellsprings of the evangelical tradition. Our failure to do so in the past has resulted in both a loss of evangelical identity and a lingering perception of the church as trite, boring and superfluous.

The evangelical witness emerged not only, and not primarily, as a protest against abuses in the church, but rather as a protest for *(pro-testantes)* the truth of the Gospel. How evangelicalism maintains the centrality of Gospel truth within ostensibly weak structures of ecclesial authority is perhaps its greatest challenge today. However, within the evangelical tradition itself, in its confessions and hymns no less than its formal theological reflections, there is a rich reservoir for articulating a strong ecclesiology in the service of the Word of God.

If it seems to Roman Catholics and other observers that evangelicals are more concerned with individualistic therapeutic spirituality than with churchly Christianity, we must admit that there is warrant for such a view. A popular book on the church, though not written by a self-professed evangelical, reflects the kind of ecclesiology found in abundance on the shelves of many Christian bookstores. Some chapter titles are: The Church as a Helpful Service Organization, The Church as an Insurance Policy, The Church Serves My Special Interests, and The Church Rescues Me in Times of Crisis.[4] More damning still is the wording posted on a sign beside an evangelical congregation: "The church that asks nothing of you!" It would be a great mistake, however, to gauge the rich tradition of evangelical ecclesiology by such trendy religious perversions. What are the lineaments of a consensual evangelical ecclesiology? We shall consider this theme under three general rubrics: the universality of the Church; the priority of the Gospel; and finally, the Church as One, Holy, Catholic, and Apostolic.[5]

## ◆◆   THE UNIVERSALITY OF THE CHURCH   ◆◆

Two classic texts from the evangelical tradition highlight the reality of the church universal. The first is Question Fifty-four in the *Heidelberg Catechism* (1563):

> What doest thou believe concerning the holy Catholic church? Answer: That out of the whole human race, from the beginning to the end of the world, the Son of God, by his Spirit and Word, gathers, defends, and preserves for himself unto everlasting life, a chosen communion in the unity of the true faith; and that I am, and forever shall remain, a living member of the same.[6]

The second definition is from the Second London Confession, a Particular Baptist statement of faith, published in 1677, which echoes the language of the Westminster Confession:

> The Catholic or universal Church, which with respect to the internal work of the Spirit, and truth of grace, may be called invisible, consists of the whole number of the elect, that have been, are, or shall be gathered into one, under Christ, the head thereof; and is the spouse, the body, the fullness of Him, that filleth all in all.[7]

Georges Florovsky, one of the most important Orthodox theologians of our day, used to say that the church is characterized by an ecumenicity in time as well as by an ecumenicity in space. This motif is deeply rooted in the patristic tradition, East and West, and was given classic expression by Saint Augustine, whom Luther referred to as "that poor, insignificant pastor of Hippo."[8] This idea is also well represented in the first two chapters of *Lumen gentium* on "The Mystery of the Church" and "The People of God." God the Father, says Vatican II, "determined to call together in a holy Church those who should believe in Christ. Already present in figure at the beginning of the world,...it will be brought to glorious completion at the end of time. At that moment, all the just from the time of Adam, 'from Abel, the just one, to the last of the elect' will be gathered together with the Father in the universal Church."[9]

The church, then, is the Body of Christ extended throughout time as well as space consisting of all persons everywhere who have been, as the Puritans would have put it, "savingly converted," that is, placed in vital union with Jesus Christ through the ministry of the Holy Spirit. *Extra ecclesiam nulla salus!* Outside of this church, which is *the* church in the most comprehensive, all-encompassing sense, there is no salvation.

This ecclesial motif is crucial for Catholic-evangelical fellowship in that it enables members of both traditions to recognize in one another, when and where God so permits it, the evident reality of God's grace among those who have trusted Jesus himself as Lord, Master, and divine Savior. To be sure, this kind of fellowship is a long, long way from "full visible unity," but it is equally distant from automatic mutual condemnation. Pope John Paul II says of those Christians who are beyond the visible boundaries of the Catholic Church, "We can say that in some real way they are joined with us in the Holy Spirit";[10] evangelicals too can declare the same concerning believing Catholics. The recognition of a shared spiritual reality leads on to activities of cooperation and joint witness, the kind of things referred to in the encyclical as "spiritual ecumenism," including the fellowship of prayer, the translation and dissemination of Holy Scripture, theological dialogues, and a common agenda of convictional (as opposed to merely prudential) cobelligerency against abortion, euthanasia, pornography, religious persecution, and the erosion of a moral base for politics, law and culture.

But evangelicals also understand the universality of the church in ways that are not compatible, or at least are less compatible, with Catholic teaching. As Avery Dulles has shown, the concept of the church as the Mystical Body of Christ was brought into the mainstream of Catholic ecclesiology by the famous encyclical of Pope Pius XII in 1943, *Mystici corporis.*[11] Although *Lumen gentium* modifies the positions taken by Pius XII in several respects, it does not retract the language of *Mystici corporis* which refers to the church *quasi altera Christi persona* ("as if it were another person of Christ").[12] While some Protestant theologians have also spoken of the church as a continuation of the Incarnation, most evangelicals recoil from such a direct identification lest the church itself be made into an object of faith alongside of Christ. Although Paul Tillich's theology can hardly be considered "orthodox" by evangelical criteria, he speaks for most, if not all, Protestants when he warns against the idolatrous temptation to put the historical church in the place of God.[13] In the New Testament the metaphor of the body of Christ describes the relationships of believers to one another (in 1 Corinthians) and to Christ (in Ephesians and Colossians, where the body is distinguished from Christ, its Head), but not to the environing world. In other words, "the body image looks inwards and upwards but not outwards."[14]

In the New Testament the church universal is depicted as a heavenly and eschatological reality, not as an earthly institution to be governed and grasped by mere mortals. The only text in the New Testament which directly refers to the church as the mother of believers is Galatians 4:26 where, in contrast to the earthly city in Judea, the church is called "the Jerusalem that is above, the heavenly Jerusalem." Another text of major importance which extends this idea is Hebrews 12:22–24: "But you have come to Mount Zion, to the heavenly Jerusalem, the city of the living God. You have come to thousands upon thousands of angels of joyful assembly, to the church (ekklesia) of the firstborn, whose names are written in heaven. You have come to God, the Judge of all men, to the spirits of righteous men made perfect, to Jesus the Mediator of a new covenant, and to the sprinkled blood that speaks a better word than the blood of Abel." Thus the church as a heavenly and eschatological entity includes the elect of all the ages: the saints of the old covenant as well as those of the new, the *ecclesia triumphans* and also the *ecclesia militans*. As a reality beyond our ken, this universal church is not at our disposal and thus we can only believe it *(credo ecclesiam)*—not believe *in* it as we believe in God the Father Almighty, Jesus Christ his only Son, and the Holy Spirit. Rather, when we confess that we "believe the church," we are bearing witness to its reality. We mean to say that we believe it exists; that we ourselves by God's grace have been

placed within it, along with all others who "bow their necks under
the yoke of Jesus Christ" (Belgic Confession, art. 28); and that the
gates of hell shall never prevail against it.

There is indeed a sure and direct connection between this
holy company of the redeemed in heaven and the pilgrim church
which struggles for its footing in the awful swellings of the Jordan
here below. It is precisely in this eschatological setting that we find
the most compelling New Testament proof text for regular church
attendance: "Let us not give up meeting together, as some are in
the habit of doing, but let us encourage one another—and all the
more as you see the Day approaching" (Heb 10:25). In Christian
worship our hearts are lifted into the heavenly sanctuary as we
share together the bread and cup of the Lord's Table in anticipa-
tion of the Marriage Supper of the Lamb. "Let us lift up our
hearts....We lift them up to the Lord!" This *sursum corda* moves
us forward in history even as it lifts us upward into heaven. There,
Calvin says, Christ has ascended, "not to possess it by himself, but
to gather you and all godly people with him."[15]

◆◆     THE PRIORITY OF THE GOSPEL     ◆◆

The concept of the invisible church has fallen onto hard times
in recent years, not only among Catholic interpreters but even
among Protestant exegetes as diverse as Karl Barth and Donald
Carson, who think it best not to apply the idea of invisibility to the
church.[16] It is easy to see why this expression gives so much offense.
The church "invisible" sounds too much like Casper the Friendly
Ghost—so ethereal, so docetic, so detached from the flow and flux
of the real stuff of ordinary life. At the time of the Reformation certain spiritualist reformers seemed to give credibility to the charge
which the Catholic polemicist Thomas Murner brought against
Luther early on, namely, that he wanted "to build a church as Plato
wants to build a state, which would be nowhere."[17] Thus Sebastian
Franck declared: "I believe that the outward church of Christ,
including all its gifts and sacraments, because of the breaking in and
laying waste by Antichrist right after the death of the apostles, went

up into heaven and lies concealed in the Spirit and in truth."[18] Other radical reformers such as Casper Schwenckfeld declared a moratorium *(Stillstand)* on the Lord's Supper, emphasizing instead the inward feeding upon the "celestial flesh" of Christ, a non-material eucharist transacted in the heart by faith *(alone!)*.

Over against these spiritualizing trends, however, Luther, Zwingli, Calvin, Bucer, Cranmer, and indeed most of the evangelical Anabaptists too, stressed the importance of the local visible congregation where, in the famous words of the Augsburg Confession, "the Word is rightly preached and the sacraments are rightly administered."[19] At the Leipzig Debate with John Eck in 1519, Luther firmly embraced the Augustinian concept of the church, reiterated in the late Middle Ages by John Wyclif and John Hus, as "the whole body of the elect *(praedestinatorum universitas)*."[20] But this concept did not prevent him from also exclaiming, "Thank God, a seven-year-old child knows what the church is, namely, holy believers and sheep who hear the voice of their Shepherd."[21]

For Luther, the Gospel, which he defined as the good news of salvation by grace alone through faith alone because of Jesus Christ alone, was constitutive for the church, not the church for the Gospel. As he wrote in the sixty-second of the Ninety-five Theses, "The true treasure of the church is the holy Gospel of the glory and the grace of God." As a doctor of Holy Scripture and as a pastor of souls, Luther revolted against the church for the sake of the church, that is, against a corrupt church for the sake of the "true, ancient church, one body and one communion of saints with the holy, universal, Christian church."[22] The idea that Luther embodied "the introspective conscience of the West" and that his lonely quest for truth propelled him into the abyss of subjectivism owes more to the romanticism of the nineteenth century and the individualism of the twentieth than to the reformer's own self-consciousness.

Luther's commitment to the Gospel led him to describe justification by faith alone as "the summary of all Christian doctrine." In 1537 he wrote, "Nothing in this article can be given up or compromised, even if heaven and earth and things temporal should be destroyed."[23] This message, far from being the result of privatized

religious experience or rebellious individualism, delivered the soul
precisely from such preoccupations by pointing to the finished work
of Christ on the cross. As Luther put it in his lectures on Galatians in
1535: "This is the reason why our theology is certain: it snatches us
away from ourselves, so that we do not depend on our own strength,
conscience, experience, person, or works, but depend on that which
is outside ourselves, that is, on the promise and truth of God, which
cannot deceive."[24]

Luther's doctrine of justification by faith alone was not a
novel teaching but one which he found scattered throughout the
writings of the early church, especially in the prayers of the saints,
and above all in the letters of Saint Paul. (Melanchthon traced the
expression *sola fide* to Saint Ambrose.)[25] But clearly this teaching
had become obscured in the intervening centuries. Luther's "dis-
covery of the Gospel" made justification by faith alone the center-
piece of Reformation ecclesiology.

In recent years justification by faith has been the subject of
extensive dialogue between Lutheran and Catholic scholars in this
country.[26] In Europe Karl Lehmann, Catholic bishop of Mainz,
and Lutheran theologian Wolfhart Pannenberg have led discussions on the condemnations of the Reformation era with respect
to justification. Out of these discussions has come a question
which could not have been asked even a generation ago: Do the
condemnations set forth in the *Decrees of the Council of Trent*
and in the *Book of Concord* still apply today?[27] It is not surprising
that proposals to reexamine the historic differences over justification have met with stern resistance from various quarters within
both the Catholic and Protestant worlds.

An evangelical commitment to the priority of the Gospel
means that justification by faith alone should remain the keryg-
matic center of our proclamation and common witness, even
though we also affirm with Calvin that "while we are justified by
faith alone, the faith that justifies is not alone." While good works
are never the condition, they are indeed the consequence of our
being declared righteous before our heavenly Father. Albert Outler
once summarized the theology of John Wesley in a way that may

capture the heart of the evangelical tradition at its best: faith alone, working by love, leading to holiness.[28]

While the biblical doctrine of justification remains the evangelical center of the visible church, we must guard against making shibboleths out of the precise formulations of Luther, Calvin, or any other human teacher. To turn justification by faith alone into justification by doctrinal precision alone is to lapse into a subtle but insidious form of justification by works. In this regard we do well to heed the words of Jonathan Edwards in his magisterial treatise on justification:

> How far a wonderful and mysterious agency of God's Spirit may so influence some men's hearts, that their practice in this regard may be contrary to their own principles, so that they shall not trust in their own righteousness, though they profess that men are justified by their own righteousness—or how far they may believe the doctrine of justification by men's own righteousness in general, and yet not believe it in a particular application of it to themselves—or how far that error which they may have been led into by education, or cunning sophistry of others, may yet be indeed contrary to the prevailing disposition of their hearts, and contrary to their practice—or how far some may seem to maintain a doctrine contrary to this gospel-doctrine of justification, that really do not, but only express themselves differently from others; or seem to oppose it through their misunderstanding of our expressions, or we of theirs, when indeed our real sentiments are the same in the main—or may seem to differ more than they do, by using terms that are without a precisely fixed and determinant meaning—or to be wide in their sentiments from this doctrine, for want of a distinct understanding of it; whose hearts, at the same time, entirely agree with it, and if once it was clearly explained to their understandings, would immediately close with it and embrace it:—how far these things may be, I will not determine; but am fully persuaded that great allowances are to be made on these and such like accounts, in innumerable instances.[29]

◆◆    ONE, HOLY, CATHOLIC, AND APOSTOLIC    ◆◆

The invisible or universal church emerges into visibility in the form of local congregations gathered around the faithful preaching of the Word of God: a community (*Gemeine* was Luther's word) or called-out assembly of the people of God, the fellowship of believers or, as the Apostles' Creed has it, the communion of saints. Thus, evangelicals can agree wholeheartedly with the statement of *Lumen gentium* that in local churches "the faithful are gathered together through the preaching of the Gospel of Christ, and the mystery of the Lord's Supper is celebrated....In these communities, though they may often be small and poor, or existing in the diaspora, Christ is present, through whose power and influence the One, Holy, Catholic, and Apostolic Church is constituted" (LG 26). The church universal and the church local are related not as two species of the same genus but rather as two predicates of the same subject. Gregory the Great declared that: "The holy church has two lives: one in time and the other in eternity."[30] The connection between the one church in its two successive states is the Holy Spirit.

### The Church Is One

The New Testament speaks of "churches" in the plural, particular congregations of baptized believers united in a common confession, sharing a mutual love for one another across the barriers of race and class, nation and "denomination" ("I am of Paul, I am of Apollos," and so on). In his letter to the Ephesians, the Magna Carta of New Testament ecclesiology, Paul makes this urgent plea: "Make every effort to keep the unity of the Spirit through the bond of peace. There is one body and one spirit—just as you were called to one hope when you were called—one Lord, one faith, one baptism; one God and Father of all, who is over all and through all and in all" (Eph 4:3–5). Thus the unity of the church is based on the fact that we worship one God. As Edmund Clowney has observed, "If we served many gods—Isis, Apollo, Dionysos, Demeter—then we might form different cults, for there were 'gods many and lords many.' But we serve the one true God, who is also the heavenly Father of his one family" (Eph 3:14).[31]

Heiko Oberman has claimed that schism was not the result of the Reformation but instead its genesis and point of departure.[32] It is clear that neither Luther nor Calvin had any idea of starting new churches; they aimed instead to reform the One, Holy, Catholic, and Apostolic Church. As Calvin put it, "To leave the church is nothing less than a denial of God and Christ *(Dei et Christi abnegatio)*."[33]

Continental Anabaptists, English Separatists, and biblical restorationists pursued a different ideal of reform, seeking not so much to purify the church as to restore it to its original, New Testament condition. Thus by gathering new congregations of "visible saints," organized according to the blueprint of church order in the New Testament, these radical reformers believed that they could restore, as one of them put it, "the old glorious face of primitive Christianity."[34] The end result of this process was the proliferation of numerous denominations and competing sects, "separated brethren" who were often more separated than brotherly in their relations with one another!

Evangelicals today are heirs of both reformational and restitutionist models of ecclesiology and their approach to controverted questions of church order, ministry, and ecumenism often depends on which of these two paradigms is more prevalent. The fact that most evangelicals are less than enthusiastic about the modern ecumenical movement in its liberal Protestant modality does not mean that they have no concern for the unity of the church. It does mean, however, that the question of the church's unity cannot be divorced from that of its integrity. The call to be one in Christ rings hollow when it comes from church leaders who either themselves deny, or wink at others who do, the most basic Christological affirmations of the Christian faith including the virgin birth, bodily resurrection and actual return of Christ himself. Thomas Oden speaks for many evangelicals when he declares: "Too many pretentious pseudoecumenical efforts have been themselves divisive, intolerant, ultrapolitical, misconceived, utopian, abusive, nationalistic, and culturally

imperialistic....Hence modern ecumenical movements are themselves called to repentance on behalf of the unity of the church.
Without true repentance, it is doubtful that the varied houses of
Protestantism can speak confidently of the one body of Christ."[35]
But evangelicals too are called to repentance. We too have sinned
against the Body of Christ by confusing loyalty to the truth with
party spirit and Kingdom advance with petty self-aggrandizement.
We need the wisdom of the Holy Spirit to know when, like the Confessing Church in Nazi Germany, it is necessary to stand against
schemes of false church unity and compromised theology to declare,
"Jesus Christ, as he is testified to us in the Holy Scripture, is the one
Word of God, whom we are to hear, whom we are to trust and obey
in life and in death."[36]

### The Church Is Holy

Of the four classic attributes of the church, holiness is the
one best attested in the most primitive versions of the baptismal
creed: "I believe in the *hagian ekklesian*," or, according to a variant tradition, "I believe *through* the holy church *(per sanctam
ecclesiam).*"[37] The church is a "called-out assembly"; it is *sanctas,*
"holy," in so far as it exists over against the surrounding culture.
The Apostle Peter addressed his first epistle to "God's elect,
strangers in the world...who have been chosen according to the
foreknowledge of God the Father through the sanctifying work of
the Spirit for obedience to Jesus Christ." To these gentile churches
scattered throughout the Roman Empire, he said, "Do not conform to the evil desires you had when you lived in ignorance. But
just as He who called you is holy, so be holy in all you do; for it is
written: 'Be holy because I am holy'" (1 Pt 1:1–2, 14–16).
The church on earth is holy not by virtue of its being set apart
from every other institution and community in its external organization, as though it were some kind of *cordon sanitaire* in the midst
of the contagion all around it, but only because it is animated by the
Holy Spirit and joined in vital union with its heavenly Head, Jesus
Christ himself. Thus Zacharias Ursinus in his *Commentary on the*

*Heidelberg Catechism* said the church "is called holy because it is sanctified of God by the blood and Spirit of Christ, that it may be conformable to him, not in perfection, but by the imputation of Christ's righteousness, or obedience; and by having the principle of holiness; because the Holy Spirit renews and delivers the church from the dregs of sins by degrees, in order that all who belong to it may commence and practice all the parts of obedience."[38]

Evangelicals insist, however, that the holiness of God be clearly distinguished from the holiness of the church. The holiness of the church on earth is entirely derived, emergent and incomplete; that of God is eternal, substantial and unbroken by the vicissitudes of imperfection and finitude. Thus we take exception to the statement of Yves Congar that "there is no more sin in the church than in Christ, of whom she is the body; and she is his mystical personality."[39] In an early draft of the section of *Lumen gentium* describing the church as the people of God, there was an acknowledgment of the sin to which the church is susceptible in its earthly pilgrimage. In the official text, however, the putative sinfulness of the church was qualified by adding the words "in its members." However, as Hans Küng has said, "There is no such thing as a church without members...it is human beings, not God, not the Lord, not the Spirit, who make up the church."[40] The justified believer is always *simul iustus et peccator,* "at the same time righteous and sinful"; and, consequently, the visible church must be at the same time a *communio peccatorum* as well as a *communio sanctorum.*

Did Luther's univocal insistence upon justification by faith alone as the center of evangelical proclamation leave no room for sanctification, good works, or growth in grace and holiness? The Catholic prince Duke George of Saxony thought so: "Luther's doctrine is good for the dying, but it is no good for the living." Erasmus was less kind: "Lutherans seek only two things—wealth and wives...to them the Gospel means the right to live as they please."[41]

While it is true that for Luther the sole, uninterrupted, and infallible mark of the church was and remained the Gospel—*ubi evangelium, ibi ecclesia*—he also has much to say about good works and growth in holiness as the fruit of having been declared righteous by God through faith alone. Later reformers placed more emphasis on the "marks of the true church" (word and sacrament for Luther and Calvin, discipline as well for later Reformed confessions, English Separatists and Anabaptists). Calvin in particular is clear about the function of the marks: "For, in order that the title 'church' may not deceive us, every congregation that claims the name 'church' must be tested by this standard as by a touchstone."[42] The evangelical marks—proclamation, worship, and discipline—are thus distinguished from the traditional Nicene attributes precisely because they are not merely descriptive, but dynamic: they call into question the unity, catholicity, apostolicity, and holiness of every congregation which claims to be a church. In this way, as Calvin says, "the face of the church" emerges into visibility before our eyes.[43]

By elevating discipline to the status of a distinguishing mark of the church, Puritans, Pietists, and the early Methodists defined the true visible church as a covenanted company of gathered saints, *separated from* the world in its organization and autonomy, and *separating back to* the world through congregational discipline those members whose lives betrayed their profession. Such procedures were meant to be remedial rather than punitive; they were intended to underscore the imperatives of life and growth within the church, understood as an intentional community of mutual service and mutual obligation by which "the whole body, bonded and knit together by every constituent joint...grows through the due activity of each part, and builds itself up" (Eph 4:16).

### The Church Is Catholic

Most evangelicals are happy to confess that the church is one, holy, and apostolic. These are, after all, not only biblical concepts but also New Testament terms. But in what sense can evangelicals affirm *credimus catholicam ecclesiam?* Although many contemporary evangelical churches have long abandoned the word *catholic,* and would even consider it an insult to be called such, and have gone so far as to alter the traditional wording of the Apostles' Creed to avoid the duty of pronouncing it, none of this changes the fact that evangelicals are indeed Catholics in so far as they believe that in its essence the Christian community is one and the same in all places and in all ages—the one, holy, universal church which embraces true believers in all sectors of human society and in all epochs of human history.[44] The reformers of the sixteenth century and the Puritans of the seventeenth, not excluding Baptists, were happy for their churches to be called Catholic (cf. Richard Baxter, *The True Catholick*, 1660).

Indeed, it is not too much to say that these evangelical forebears opposed the Church of Rome not because it was too Catholic, but because it was not Catholic enough. They spoke of the evidence for catholicity in three respects: its geographical extent, the church as spread over the whole world, not restricted to any particular place, kingdom, or nation; its inclusive membership, gathered from all classes and ranks of human society; and its indefectibility, based on the promise of the risen Christ: "I will be with you always even to the end of the world" (Mt 28:20).[45]

Evangelical expositors, however, were careful not to define true catholicity in terms of quantifiable, empirical evidence alone. Ecclesiastical longevity can be deceptive for, as the Scots Confession of 1560 pointed out, Cain, with respect to age and title, was preferred to both Abel and Seth.[46] So, too, historical continuity, numerical quantity, and cultural variety do not themselves constitute true catholicity. The true church may be quite small: Where two or three of you are gathered together in my name, Jesus said, there I am in your midst. This "I" is the only basis of true catholicity. As Barth puts it, "The Real Church is the assembly which is called, united, held together and governed by the Word of her Lord, or she is not the Real Church."[47]

In contemporary evangelical life, perhaps the most notable aspect of catholicity is the worldwide missionary vision which is the heart and soul of the evangelical movement. Indeed, what ecumenism is to post-Vatican II Catholicism, missions and world evangelization are for evangelicalism, not an appendix added to church activity, but an organic part of its life and work. The

importance of declaring the Gospel to those who have never heard
it was at the heart of William Carey's mission to India in 1793, an
event which launched what Kenneth Scott Latourette called "the
great century" of Protestant missionary advance.[48] This witness
continues today through the mission boards of evangelical
denominations and a vast network of international parachurch
ministries such as the Billy Graham Evangelistic Association,
Campus Crusade for Christ, World Vision, and Prison Fellowship.
The evangelical understanding of catholicity is nowhere better
seen than in this world Christian movement through which
redeemed saints "from every tribe and language and people and
nation" are being gathered by God's grace into that heavenly cho-
rus to sing with the angels, martyrs and all the saints: "The Lamb
is worthy—the Lamb who was slain. He is worthy to receive
power and riches and wisdom and strength and honor and glory
and blessing" (Rv 5:9, 12).

## The Church Is Apostolic

Because the church is One, Holy and Catholic, it is also Apostolic, a word added to the Nicene description of the church in 381
but clearly expressed already in Paul's metaphor of the church as
"God's house, built on the foundation of the apostles and the
prophets, and the cornerstone is Christ Jesus himself" (Eph 2:20).
That church is apostolic which stands under the direction and normative authority of the apostles, whom Jesus chose and sent forth in
his Name. Evangelicals, no less than Roman Catholics, claim to be
apostolic in this sense, but the two traditions differ sharply on the
way in which they understand the transmission of the apostolic witness from the first century until now.

Catholics believe that the church continues to be "taught,
sanctified, and guided by the apostles...through their successors in
pastoral office: the college of bishops, assisted by priests, in union
with the successor of Peter, the church's supreme pastor." As the
*Catechism of the Catholic Church* puts it, "The bishops have by
divine institution taken the place of the apostles as pastors of the

Church, in such wise that whoever listens to them is listening to Christ and whoever despises them despises Christ and Him who sent Christ."[49] As heirs of the Reformation, evangelicals do not define the apostolicity of the church in terms of a literal, linear succession of duly ordained bishops. They point instead to the primordial character of the Gospel, the inscripturated witness of the apostles, and the succession of apostolic proclamation.

While the church is indeed built on the foundation of the holy apostles, and their predecessors, the prophets, there is something more basic and more important than even these worthy servants, namely, the message they proclaimed: Jesus Christ and Him crucified. This is a constant note throughout the ministry of Paul who wrote to the Corinthians, "For we do not preach ourselves, but Jesus Christ as Lord, and ourselves as your servants for Jesus' sake" (2 Cor 4:5). Again, in writing to the Galatians, when his own apostolic authority was under severe attack, Paul appeals to an authority beyond himself—the Gospel. "But even if we or an angel from heaven should preach a gospel other than the one we preach to you let him be eternally condemned!" (Gal 1:8). Paul brought himself under his own curse: *"But even if we...."* Paul did not ask the Galatians to be loyal to him but rather to the unchanging message of Christ, Christ alone, that he had preached to them.

In a different form, this same issue would surface again during the Donatist controversy. The question was whether religious rites such as baptism, the Lord's Supper, and ordination could be valid and effective when performed by a minister who was morally impure. Augustine argued that the sacraments were effective by virtue of the power invested in them by Christ himself and the promise of his Word. At the time of the Reformation, this issue came under review again, and the essential point of the Augustinian position was recognized as valid: the true touchstone of doctrinal and spiritual authenticity is God himself, what he has irrevocably done in Christ and vouchsafed to us in Holy Scripture, not the qualifications, charisma, or even theology of any human leader.[50] As the authorized representatives of Jesus Christ, the apostles have faithfully and accurately transmitted their authoritative witness to their

Lord in the divinely inspired writings of Holy Scripture. The teaching authority of the apostles thus resides in the canonical scriptures of the Old and New Testaments, the self-authenticating Word of God, the truth of which is confirmed in the believer by the illuminating witness of the Holy Spirit.

For evangelicals the principle of *sola Scriptura* means that all the teachings, interpretations, and traditions of the church must be subjected to the divine touchstone of Holy Scripture itself. But *sola Scriptura* is not *nuda Scriptura*. Evangelicals cannot accept the idea of tradition as a coequal or supplementary source of revelation, but neither can we ignore the rich exegetical tradition of the early Christian writers whose wisdom and insight is vastly superior to the latest word from today's guilded scholars. The consensus of thoughtful Christian interpretation of the Word down the ages (and on most matters of importance there is such a thing) is not likely to be wrong, and evangelicals, no less than other Christians, have much to learn from the church fathers, schoolmen, and theologians of ages past.[51]

Even before their inspired message was committed to writing, the apostles were effectively proclaiming the Good News of Jesus Christ throughout the Roman Empire. Thus, Paul said to the Ephesians, "Remember that for three years I never stopped warning each of you night and day with tears" (Acts 20:31). To the Thessalonians he recalled how "our Gospel came to you not simply with words, but also with power with the Holy Spirit and with deep conviction" (1 Thes 1:5). For evangelicals, public preaching of the Word of God is a sure sign of apostolicity for through the words of the preacher, the living voice of the Gospel *(viva vox evangelii)* is heard. The church, Luther said, is not a "pen house" but a "mouth house." The Second Helvetic Confession (1566) goes so far as to say that "the preaching of the Word of God is the Word of God." The almost sacramental quality of preaching in the evangelical tradition has sometimes obscured the importance of the "visible words" of God in baptism and the Lord's Supper. Vatican II's "Instruction on the Proper Implementation of the Constitution on the Sacred Liturgy" recognized that "it is especially necessary that there be close links between liturgy, catechesis, religious instruction and preaching."[52] Evangelicals, no less than Catholics, should strive for a proper balance among these constituent acts of worship. In doing so, however, evangelicals must not compromise the priority of proclamation for today, as in the time of the apostles: "God is pleased through the foolishness of what is preached to save those who believe" (1 Cor 1:21).[53]

<h2>◆◆    ECCLESIA IN VIA CRUCIS    ◆◆</h2>

"I believe in one, holy, catholic and apostolic church," Archbishop William Temple once remarked, "but regret that it doesn't exist."[54] To which the evangelical responds: If by "exist" we mean perfect, complete, unbroken, infallibly secure, verifiably visible in its external structures and temporal resources, then it is clear that such a church does not exist in this world. Furthermore, if, after a thorough investigation, a panel of ecumenical experts, well trained in the latest techniques of sociological research, were to announce at a press conference that they had at long last found such a church, then nothing in heaven and earth would be more certain than that *that* church could not be the One, Holy, Catholic and Apostolic Church founded by Jesus Christ. In this life the true church is always *ecclesia in via (Kirche im Werden),* the church in a state of becoming, buffeted by struggles, beset by the eschatological "groanings" which mark those "upon whom the ends of the world have come" (Rom 8:18–25; 1 Cor 10:11).

In 1525 Luther wrote a lyrical hymn praising the church:

To me she's dear, the worthy maid, and I cannot forget her;
Praise, honor, virtue of her are said; then all I love her better.

On earth, all mad with murder, the mother now alone is she,
But God will watchful guard her, and the right Father be.[55]

To the eyes of faith the church is a "worthy maid," the Bride of Christ, but by the standards of the world she is a poor Cinderella surrounded by numerous dangerous foes:

> If, then, a person desires to draw the church as he sees her, he
> will picture her as a deformed and poor girl sitting in an
> unsafe forest in the midst of hungry lions, bears, wolves, and
> boars, nay, deadly serpents; in the midst of infuriated men
> who set sword, fire, and water in motion in order to kill her
> and wipe her from the face of the earth.[56]

In God's sight the church is pure, holy, unspotted, the dove of
God; but in the eyes of the world, it bears the form of a servant. It
is like its Bridegroom, Christ: "hacked to pieces, marked with
scratches, despised, crucified, mocked" (Is 53:2–3).[57]

It is only from a posture of ecclesial vulnerability that evangelicals and Catholics can be able to reach out to one another
across the great divide which still separates us. Only in this way
can we, believing Catholics and confessional evangelicals, reach
out to one another in openness and love, the kind of love which is
not puffed up, seeketh not its own; the kind of love which rejoices
not in iniquity, but rejoices in the truth and, for this very reason, is
able then to bear all things, believe all things, hope all things and
endure all things. Only in this way will we be able really to hear
one another and thus to avoid what Cardinal Cassidy has aptly
called "the dialogue of the deaf." For evangelicals to imagine that
nothing has changed in Catholicism since the Council of Trent,
and for Catholics to see evangelicals as rebellious sects who must
return, like prodigal sons, to the haven of Rome, is to engage in a
dialogue of the deaf. We will not break down the walls of division
and distrust in this way.

As evangelicals and Catholics pursue theological dialogue,
moved by our love for the truth and our love for one another, we
must not let our discussions degenerate into a kind of armchair
ecumenism—heady, aloof, and divorced from an awareness of
"the pestilence that walks in darkness, and the destruction that
wastes at noonday" (Ps 91:6). We have been brought together by
what I have called elsewhere "an ecumenism of the trenches." We
are comrades in a struggle, not a struggle against one another, and
not a struggle against men and women outside the Christian faith
who reject the light of divine grace because they have fallen in love

with the darkness which surrounds them; no, our conflict is against the Prince of Evil himself, against the cosmic powers and potentates of this dark world. For the church, much more is at stake than who comes out on top in the current "culture wars." All of our programs and plans will ring hollow unless we stand in solidarity with our brothers and sisters in Christ, evangelicals and Catholics alike, who live under the shadow of the cross and whose faithful witness is even now leading many of them to the shedding of their blood. Throughout *Ut unum sint,* Pope John Paul II calls us to remember "the courageous witness of so many martyrs of our century, including members of churches and ecclesial communities not in full communion with the Catholic Church."[58]

More than a decade before the convening of Vatican II, a Southern Baptist medical missionary, Dr. Bill Wallace, along with two Roman Catholic missionaries, Bishop Donaghy and Sister Rosalia of the Maryknolls, were arrested by Communist thugs and brutally mistreated because of their Christian faith. Dr. Wallace was eventually killed by his captors. Following his death, Thomas Brack, leader of the Maryknoll Mission, sent the following letter to the Southern Baptist Foreign Mission Board:

> The Maryknoll fathers of the Wuchow Diocese mourn the loss of Dr. Wallace whose friendship they esteem. He healed our malaria, our skin ulcers, and the other illnesses that missioners manage to pick up. He will be mourned by thousands of Chinese, at whose bedside he sat and in whose eyes his name will always bring a light of gratitude, though governments may come and go.[59]

On another continent, in a different war, the cost of discipleship was no less dear. Several years ago on a visit to Germany, I was taken to what remains of the concentration camp at Buchenwald near Weimar. Here more than sixty-five thousand people were put to death by a totalitarian regime which saw in the Christian faith, in both its Catholic and Protestant expressions, a threat to the ideology of death. At Buchenwald there was one block of cells reserved for prisoners deemed especially dangerous or notable. In cell 27 they placed Paul Schneider, a Lutheran pastor, who was called "the Preacher of Buchenwald" because even from the small window in his cell he loudly proclaimed the Gospel of Jesus Christ in defiance of the orders of the Gestapo guards. In cell 23 they placed Otto Neururer, a Catholic priest, whose work on behalf of the Jews and other so-called "undesirables" had made him a threat to the Nazi warlords. He too ministered in Jesus' Name to his fellow inmates in the concentration camp. In Buchenwald a son of Rome and a son of the Reformation, separated no longer by four centuries but only by four cells, walked the *via crucis* and bore witness together to their common Lord, Jesus Christ, the sole and sufficient Redeemer. As evangelicals and Catholics together, we remember them and give thanks to God for them, and for countless others like them, who share a *koinonia* in the sufferings of Jesus, for today, as in ages past, the blood of the martyrs is the seed of the church—the One, Holy, Catholic, and Apostolic Church.

*IPSI GLORIA IN ECCLESIA.*
AMEN.

### Notes

1. Cited in Eberhard Bethge, *Dietrich Bonhoeffer* (New York: Harper & Row, 1970), 42. Cf. Bonhoeffer's doctoral dissertation, first published in 1930, on the doctrine of the church, *The Communion of Saints* (New York: Harper & Row, 1960).

2. Donald A. Carson "Evangelicals, Ecumenism, and the Church," in *Evangelical Affirmations*, ed. Kenneth S. Kantzer and Carl F. H. Henry (Grand Rapids: Zondervan, 1900), 355.

3. J. C. Hoekendijk, "The Church in Missionary Thinking," *The International Review of Missions* 41 (1952), 325.

4. Barbara Brown Zikmund, *Discovering the Church* (Philadelphia: Westminster Press, 1983).

5. D. A. Carson has taken a complementary approach in defining evangelical ecclesiology in terms of seven basic theses: (1) The church is the community of the new covenant; (2) The church is the community empowered by the Holy Spirit; (3) The church is an eschatological community; (4) The church is the "gathered" people of God; (5) The church

is a worshiping community; (6) The church is the product of God's gracious self-disclosure in revelation and redemption; (7) The church is characterized by mission. See his *Evangelicals, Ecumenism, and the Church*, 358–371.

6. Philip Schaff, ed., *Creeds of Christendom* (New York: Harper & Brothers, 1877), 3:324–325.

7. In 1742 this same Confession was published in America, with slight alterations, as the Philadelphia Confession of Faith. Cf. Timothy and Denise George, eds., *Baptist Confessions, Covenants, and Catechisms* (Nashville: Broadman & Holman, 1996), 84–85.

8. Georges Florovsky, "The Quest for Christian Unity and the Orthodox Church," *Theology and Life* 4 (1961), 201. WA 50, 615 (WML 5,252).

9. *Lumen gentium* 2; Austin Flannery, ed., *Vatican Council II: The Conciliar and Postconciliar Documents* (Collegeville: Liturgical Press, 1975), 351.

10. *Ut unum sint*, 53.

11. Avery Dulles, *Models of the Church*, expanded Image Books ed. (New York: Doubleday, 1987) 52.

12. Quoted from Paul Schrotenboer (ed.), *Roman Catholicism: A Contemporary Evangelical Perspective* (Grand Rapids: Baker Book House, 1988), 21. However, the following statement in *Lumen gentium* 8 does not equate, but only compares the church and the Incarnation: "For this reason the church is compared, not without significance, to the mystery of the incarnate Word. As the assume nature, inseparably united to him, serves the divine Word as a living organ of salvation, so, in a somewhat similar way, does the social structure of the Church serve the spirit of Christ who vivifies it, in the building up of the body (cf. Eph. 4:15)" (Flannery, 357).

13. Paul Tillich, *Systematic Theology* (Chicago: The University of Chicago Press, 1963), 3:162–182.

14. P. T. O'Brien, "The Church as a Heavenly and Eschatological Entity," in *The Church in the Bible and the World: An International Study*, ed. by D. A. Carson (Grand Rapids: Baker Book House, Paternoster Press, 1993), 113–114.

15. John Calvin, *Institutes of the Christian Religion* 4.17. 29.

16. Richard John Neuhaus speaks thus about the importance of ecclesiology in evangelical-Catholic dialogue: "It is a question of *the* Church as such. Not an invisible church or a church of true believers that

is conceptually removed from the ambiguities and tragedies of history, but the Church that is this identifiable people through time, a people as vulnerable to the real world of historical change as was, and is, their crucified Lord." *Evangelicals and Catholics Together: Toward a Common Mission*, ed. by Charles Colson and Richard John Neuhaus (Dallas: Word, 1995), 191–192.

17. WA 7, 683, 11. Cited in Werner Elert, *The Structure of Lutheranism* (St. Louis: Concordia Publishing House, 1962), 261.

18. George H. Williams, ed., *Spiritual and Anabaptist Writers* (Philadelphia: Westminster Press, 1957), 149.

19. "The church is the assembly of saints in which the Gospel is taught purely and the sacraments are administered rightly." *The Book of Concord*, ed. Theodore G. Tappert (Philadelphia: Fortress Press, 1959), 32. On the Anabaptist view of the church, see Franklin H. Littell, *The Origins of Sectarian Protestantism* (New York: Macmillan, 1964), and Arnold Snyder, *The Life and Thought of Michael Sattler* (Scottdale, Pa.: Herald Press, 1984).

20. WA 2, 287, 35.

21. *Book of Concord*, 315.

22. LW 41, 119.

23. WA 25, 357; 50, 119. See Timothy George, *Theology of the Reformers* (Nashville: Broadman & Holman, 1988), 62–79.

24. LW 26, 387.

25. *Book of Concord*, 31–32. Hans Küng notes many other citations of *fides sola* in pre-Reformation writings. See his *Justification: The Doctrine of Karl Barth and a Catholic Reflection* (London: Thomas Nelson, 1964), 249–263.

26. See H. George Anderson, et al., eds., *Justification By Faith: Lutherans and Catholics in Dialogue VII* (Minneapolis: Augsburg Publishing House, 1985).

27. Karl Lehmann and Wolfhart Pannenberg, eds., *The Condemnations of the Reformation Era: Do They Still Divide?* (Minneapolis: Fortress Press, 1990).

28. Cf. Albert C. Outler, ed., *John Wesley* (New York: Oxford University Press, 1964), 28: "The faith that justifies bears its fruits in the faith that works by love."

29. *The Works of Jonathan Edwards* (Edinburgh: Banner of Truth, 1974) 1: 654.

30. Gregory the Great, *In Ezech.* 2, 10 (PL 76, 1060). Cited in Henri de Lubac, *The Splendor of the Church* (San Francisco: Ignatius Press, 1986 [ET 1956]), 78.

31. Edmund P. Clowney, *The Church* (Downers Grove, Ill.: Inter-Varsity Press, 1995), 79.

32. Heiko A. Oberman, *Luther: Man Between God and the Devil* (New Haven: Yale University Press, 1982), 249.

33. John Calvin, *Institutes* 4.3.2.

34. See Timothy George, "The Spirituality of the Radical Reformation," *Christian Spirituality: High Middle Ages and Reformation*, ed. Jill Raitt (New York: Crossroad, 1987), 334–371.

35. Thomas C. Oden, *Life in the Spirit* (San Francisco: Harper-Collins, 1992), 309.

36. "The Barmen Declaration," in *Creeds of the Churches*, ed. John H. Leith (Atlanta: John Knox Press, 1982), 520.

37. Oden, *Life in the Spirit*, 316.

38. Zacharias Ursinus, *Commentary on the Heidelberg Catechism* (Phillipsburg, New Jersey: Presbyterian and Reformed Publishing Company, 1992), 289.

39. Yves Congar, *Sainte Église* (1963), pp. 144ff. Cited in G. C. Berkouwer, *The Church* (Grand Rapids: Eerdmans, 1976), 341.

40. Küng, *The Church*, 415–416; Clowney, *The Church*, 86.

41. P. S. Allen and H. M. Allen, eds., *Opus Epistolarum Des Erasmi Roterodami* (Oxford: Oxford University Press, 1928), 7, 366.

42. Calvin, *Institutes* 4. 1. 11.

43. Calvin, *Institutes* 4. 1. 9.

44. This point is elaborated most effectively in Oden, *Life in the Spirit*, 337–349. See also Küng, *The Church*, 383–411; Clowney, *The Church*, 90–98.

45. Ursinus, *Commentary on the Heidelberg Catechism*, 289–290.

46. Schaff, *Creeds of Christendom,* 3:461.

47. Karl Barth, "The Real Church," *Scottish Journal of Theology* (1950), 337–351.

48. Kenneth Scott Latourette, *A History of Christianity* (New York: Harper & Row, 1953). See also Timothy George, *Faithful Witness: The Life and Mission of William Carey* (Birmingham: New Hope Press, 1991).

49. *Catechism of the Catholic Church* (Washington: United States Catholic Conference, 1994), 227–229.

50. On the significance of the Donatist controversy in the history of Christian thought, see Jaraslav Pelikan, *The Emergence of the Catholic Tradition (100–600)* (Chicago: University of Chicago Press, 1971), 307–318. See also Timothy George, *Galatians* (Nashville: Broadman & Holman, 1994), 96–98.

51. In writing against the Anabaptists in 1528, Luther said: "We do not reject everything that is under the dominion of the Pope. For in that event we should also reject the Christian church. Much Christian good is found in the papacy and from there it descended to us." LW 40, 231.

52. "Instruction on the Proper Implementation of the Constitution on the Sacred Liturgy," no. 7; Flannery, 46.

53. In what is quite a remarkable statement from an evangelical theologian, Wayne Grudem concedes that on the basis of pure preaching of the Word of God and an acceptable sacramental practice, true churches may be found within the established structures of Roman Catholicism. Wayne Grudem, *Systematic Theology: An Introduction to Biblical Doctrine* (Grand Rapids: Zondervan, 1994), 866. On the possibility of true churches in Roman obedience, Grudem, it seems, has Calvin on his side. "Therefore," wrote the Genevan reformer, "while we are unwilling simply to concede the name of Church to the papists, we do not deny that there are churches among them" (*Institutes* 4. 2. 12). See Alexandre Ganoczy, *The Young Calvin* (Philadelphia: Westminster Press, 1987), 266–286.

54. Cited in George Carey, *A Tale of Two Churches* (Downers Grove, Ill.: InterVarsity Press, 1985), 147.

55. LW 53, 293. This hymn is based on the text in Revelation 12:1–2 which describes a woman suffering in childbirth, which Luther interpreted as the church under assault by Satan.

56. WA 40/3, 315.

57. LW 54, 262.

58. *Ut unum sint*, 49.

59. Jesse C. Fletcher, *Bill Wallace of China* (Nashville: Broadman & Holman, 1996), 241.

*Chapter 7*

# When Obedience Leads Us into the Unknown

*David E. Bjork*

    I still remember my disappointment when I began to realize that God was leading me to a life of missionary service in France. The problem was not that I resisted the idea of being a missionary. That was an issue that I had settled years before at a Christian youth camp. No, the problem was not the missionary call, the problem was the particular mission field. The problem was France!

    Ever since I first felt God's call to missionary service I envisioned serving Him in some Third World country. The biographies of Christian men and women who had trekked through steamy jungles to bring the gospel message to an isolated tribe, translated the Scriptures into some unwritten language, founded hospitals, schools and suffered unimaginable hardships for Christ gave me an idea of what missionary life was all about. Moreover, as far as I was concerned, missionaries are individuals who go to isolated parts of the globe to announce Christ to peoples who have never heard His name. Had not the apostle Paul established the model for missions when he wrote: "It has always been my ambition to preach the gospel where Christ was not known, so that I would not be building on someone else's foundation" (Rom 15:20)? I did not see how France could be considered a mission field.

There are a number of things about the idea of missionary service in France that bothered me. France is the most touristic of European countries. Who ever heard of being a missionary in the same place where well-to-do westerners take their vacations? Moreover, France is a rich and industrious nation and the French are sophisticated, well educated, and technologically advanced. They have no need of missionary schools, hospitals, or linguistic work. Besides, I wondered, isn't France a part of Christian Europe? Isn't the Judeo-Christian culture of North America a result, at least in part, of the missionary efforts of the French some 250 years ago? How can one go as a missionary to a country once known as the "eldest daughter of the church"? Is it legitimate to send missionaries to a land that has been associated with the Christian faith for the past 2000 years, and from which the message of Christ continues to be sent out to the "not yet fully missionized lands"?

While I was mulling over these questions I was further troubled by an encounter with an Evangelical Protestant missions expert in Southern California. Through a study of the world-wide expansion of the church, this well-intentioned individual had come to realize that the Christian faith has fixed itself at different periods of time in different heartlands, waning in one as it has come to birth in another. Based on that observation, his counsel to me was: "Dave, the Holy Spirit is not working in France today. He is involved in a mighty way in other parts of the world. Don't waste your time in France; go to an area of the world where He is already at work, and join in what He is doing." These words reminded me of the harsh judgment expressed by a Dutch immigrant to North America: "Dave," he said, "the French have had their chance! When they rejected the Reformation they rejected God. He is no longer working in their country."

In spite of these objections and my own hesitations, God continued to deepen my conviction that He had not only called me to a life of missionary service, but to missionary service *in France.*

◆◆    CHURCH-PLANTING IN FRANCE    ◆◆

In 1979 my wife and I were commissioned as "church planters" to France for World Partners, the missionary arm of the Missionary Church, an Evangelical denomination. When we first set out on our missionary enterprise we only had a vague idea of how God might lead us to minister in France. However, we fixed as our objective the "development of Christian communities in France characterized by common purpose, mutual involvement in each other's lives, and group worship." Although we were not altogether certain as to the structure that these Christian communities would adopt, we felt that they would probably be largely like what we had experienced in the United States. Our missionary goal was the result of three different foundational convictions: (1) France can be considered a mission field because the Roman Catholic Church has compromised the Christian faith; (2) the churches that result from our ministry should not be dependent on the supporting home church, overly protected by the mother denomination, and unable to stand alone in their society; and (3) the churches that result from our ministry should be growing and multiplying groups of believers. Let's take a few minutes to look at these three foundational convictions in detail.

### 1. Roman Catholic France Is a Mission Field

I don't remember having any significant relationships with Roman Catholics as I was growing up. I can't recall ever hearing a sermon preached that mentioned Roman Catholics by name. Nor did I receive any systematic instruction about the Catholic faith. In spite of that lack of concrete information, I had formed a pretty strong conviction that Catholics did not know God as I do because of the grave errors in their doctrine. For example, I believed that: Catholics deny the resurrection (because Christ is still on their crucifixes); Catholics believe they must earn their way into heaven through good works; Catholic believers don't feel the need to pursue holy living; they simply go to confession before Mass; Catholics worship Mary; Catholics believe that they are recrucifying Christ at the Mass; Catholics believe that the Pope is infallible. I was not militantly anti-Catholic; I simply wrote the Catholic Church off as an invalid expression of Christianity and went about my business as though Catholics didn't exist.

In considering mission work in France I was obliged to acknowledge the overwhelming presence of the Roman Catholic Church in that country. There are Roman Catholic churches, many of them centuries old, in every town and village. And, all the studies indicate that almost seventy percent of the entire French population continues to consider itself Roman Catholic. However, these same studies reveal that most of these individuals do not practice their faith. Even if I had understood Roman Catholicism to be a valid expression of the Christian faith, which I didn't, the fact that most of the French are nominal believers meant that I could see them as valid targets for my missionary activities.

## 2. The Indigenous Church Principles

The second foundational premise of our church-planting ministry in France grew out of the *Indigenous Church Principles* advocated by both Henry Venn of the English Church Missionary Society and Rufus Anderson of the American Board of Commissioners for Foreign Missions. These principles, which came into their own after World War II, are summarized by Anderson: "The grand object of foreign missions is to plant and multiply churches, composed of native converts, each church complete in itself, with presbyters of the same race, left to determine their ecclesiastical relations for themselves, with the aid of judicious advice from their missionary fathers."[1]

Based on our understanding of these principles we felt that a valid goal of our missionary endeavors was the establishment of self-governing, self-supporting, and self-propagating bodies of Christian believers in France. Since we judged Roman Catholicism to be an inappropriate form of Christianity, we felt that it was necessary to establish new, independent fellowships of believers based on what we considered to be was a proper biblical understanding of the first-century church. Because most French Catholics are nominal Christians, we were convinced that new, more dynamic forms of worship, like those we had experienced in North American Evangelical Protestant circles, were necessary to draw people into the church.

## 3. The Church Growth Movement

Amplifying our conviction that we should plant new churches in France was a movement that swept through the Evangelical Protestant community in North America in the 1960s and 1970s. This current of missions thinking, fathered by Donald A. McGavran, came to be called the *Church Growth Movement*. Much of its energy was spent on discerning factors of church growth informed by the behavioral sciences, especially cultural anthropology and sociology. The basic premise underlying this movement was that churches which were not growing—and they were legion—needed to wake up to the possibilities, and get a sound biblical conscience on finding the lost. Rooted in biblical, Evangelical, conversionist theology, this movement sought to provide answers to the following question: "In a world of hundreds of millions without Christ, how can the Churches and their assisting missions achieve adequate church growth?"[2]

When linked to the *Indigenous Church Principles*, the Church Growth Movement helped me (and an entire generation of Evangelical Protestant missionaries) to understand that for the welfare of the world and for the good of humanity, according to the Bible one task is paramount. We understood that the supreme task of missions is the effective multiplication of indigenous churches in the societies of the world. The consensus of leading Evangelical Protestant missiologists is that evangelization means that every group of people should have access to an understandable hearing of the gospel *and* what the missiologists consider to be a viable, evangelizing New Testament Church.

Hence we began our ministry in France armed with the conviction that our ministry goal of leading French men and women to personal faith in Christ and banding them together to give birth to self-supporting, self-governing and self-propagating Evangelical churches was the correct missional response to the French situation. We assumed that the church either did not exist in France, or that if it did exist, it was so weakened and compromised by its history that it should be replaced. Although the strategies developed by the Church Growth Movement had met with very limited success in France, our commitment to the objective of planting independent Evangelical churches was unshaken.

In addition, the fact that Europeans recognized the need for missionaries in their lands strengthened our resolve. When Emmanuel Suhard became Archbishop of Reims in 1930, he resolutely rejected the view that French culture was Christian. He observed that the masses were largely outside the church and he recognized that the traditional methods on which the church had long relied were discredited precisely with these people. He commissioned surveys that showed plainly that France contained regions that were totally unchurched and resistant to the church, although the adjoining province or region might be a stronghold of traditional Catholic religion.

Shortly after being made cardinal archbishop of Paris in 1940, Suhard founded the *Mission de France* with the intention of training missionaries for service in France. He encouraged Abbe Godin to get on with what would eventually become the worker-priest movement. Godin was coauthor of the controversial book, *France, A Mission Land?* (1943) which put forth a vision shared by Cardinal Suhard for the primary evangelization of France. This book, along with an awareness of a growing ferment within Francophone circles, partly in response to the appeal of Pope John Paul II for the "re-evangelization" of Europe, were signs that even the Catholic Church recognized France to be a "mission field."

◆◆   STRANGE ENCOUNTERS   ◆◆

"No way," I thought. "There is no way that I am going to go with Marc and Henri to church!" What a weird situation! Under normal circumstances I wouldn't have thought twice about accompanying my young friends to church. After all, I have attended church services all of my life. But that spring day in 1981 was different. On that day the thought of going with these guys gave me knots in my stomach. No, I really didn't want to go.

At first glance the situation seems ironic. I was reared in a conservative, "Bible-believing," Evangelical Protestant home. And for as long as I can remember, I was present at church whenever its doors were open. Even during my teen years I found my sense of identity and purpose in my church relationships. Moreover, at a Christian youth camp I had responded positively when I sensed God calling me to a life of missionary service. It was obedience to that missionary call that brought me to my crisis in 1981.

Two years earlier, my wife and I, along with our four-year-old daughter and two-year-old son, had moved to the Normandy region of northwest France to begin a "church-planting ministry." After settling in an apartment in a city of about 100,000 people, I began a small Bible discussion group with some students at the local university. What an interesting group of young men they were. If they had been asked to identify themselves, the majority of them would have said something like this: "I am French. I am Catholic. I believe in reincarnation. I am an atheist. I am a scientist. I go to a healer when I am sick. I am a rationalist."

As you can no doubt imagine, we had some very engaging discussions on the life and words of Jesus as recorded in the Gospel of John. Only one or two of these young men claimed to have ever opened a Bible. Only one of them was a regular attendee at his local Catholic parish church. None of them had ever before investigated the gospel account in this kind of environment.

Over a period of several months we met and slowly progressed through the Gospel. It was exciting to watch each week as these men grappled with the fantastic claims of Jesus of Nazareth. One evening, after our study, Marc and Henri approached me with the request that I accompany them to church the following Sunday.

So here I was faced with a dilemma. These university students were just beginning to come to grips with the person and teachings of Jesus. Their new discoveries had apparently sparked in them a desire to worship. Consequently, they wanted to go to church for the first time since they were children. The only problem was that I had not yet begun the church that I had been sent to France to "start." Besides, Marc and Henri didn't want to just go to *a* church; they wanted to go to *their* church. These guys had been faithfully attending my study and now they were looking to me for reassurance and guidance. Hesitantly, reluctantly, even fearfully perhaps, I gave in to their urgings.

## A Painful Discovery

I will never forget the mixed emotions that I felt when I first entered *l'Église St. Pierre*. Although I had previously visited several cathedrals and church buildings in France, I had never attended Mass and didn't really know what to expect. The first thing that struck me was the large number of people present at the Mass. The church was packed with between 600 and 650 people. This was unheard of in our area! In fact, I was later informed that just three years earlier there were only around fifty people who regularly attended Mass in this same parish. Here, to my amazement, was a church service that was full of people.

I also felt very uncomfortable in the liturgical setting. It was a completely foreign environment to me, and I never knew when I was to sit or stand (it seemed that the Catholics were continually changing their position), or when to speak or be silent. I had a difficult time following along in the Missal, and couldn't even join in reciting the Lord's Prayer (this was not something that I had memorized in French). I felt like a fish out of water.

As real as this discomfort was, it was insignificant compared to the devastating experience that took place in the middle of Mass. What occurred hit me so powerfully that I began to tremble. We were standing, in prayer, when suddenly, unexpectedly, I began to sense the presence of God's Spirit. What I was sensing couldn't be true! *God was not supposed to be there!* Everything that I had been taught, everything that I had taught others, said that God would not be present at a Roman Catholic Mass! In other words, I believed that God could go to Mass to convict someone of their sinfulness and need of the Savior, but He wouldn't hang around afterwards! My theological convictions were that God's Spirit should not be at a Roman Catholic Mass.

When we left Mass I told my wife, "I am never going to go to Mass again! I don't like what I felt in there!"

A couple of weeks later another member of our Bible study group "took me by the hand" and led me back to Mass at St. Peter's. Once again I was overwhelmed during the Mass by a sense of God's presence. I imagine that what I felt must have been similar to the emotions Peter experienced when the Holy Spirit fell on Cornelius and his household *before* he had a chance to finish his sermon (Acts 10:44). Peter must have wondered how God could be so quick to give His Spirit to this Roman. This soldier. Peter hadn't had the time to "straighten him out." The Scriptures don't even indicate that Cornelius had time to "repent" and be "converted" (although I am sure that this actually took place). As had happened with Peter in his relationship to Cornelius, God sneaked up on me and surprised me by His grace to an "outsider."

Now, I should remind you that I come from a conservative Evangelical Protestant background. I have been taught not to put my trust in what I feel or sense. So when the conflict came between what I was "sensing" and what I "knew to be true," I automatically favored the discernment of my mind. At the same time, in my spirit I was deeply troubled. At the end of the second experience of the Mass I felt led to get together with the parish priest to see if I couldn't sort out some of these things.

We met in Father Norbert's office the following afternoon. During the three or four hours together I shared with him the story that you have just finished reading. He graciously listened, and then shared his own testimony with me. After I had asked him some specific questions concerning doctrines over which our churches are in disagreement, we spent some time in prayer.

This meeting with Father Norbert only deepened my confusion. I continued to sense that I was in the presence of a man in whom dwelt the Spirit of the living God. As I listened to his testimony I could identify specific moments of conversion in his life, and his devotion to our Lord Jesus Christ came through loud and clear. At the same time, he held beliefs that I couldn't accept. How could this be? Was I reading him correctly? At times I felt that we were saying the same things, and at others I sensed that we were in completely different worlds.

In order to try to discern more clearly what was going on I asked if Father Norbert would meet with me for prayer once a week. As a result we met and prayed together nearly every Wednesday morning for three and a half years. Sometimes we prayed together for fifteen or twenty minutes; sometimes this time of sharing and prayer took the entire morning.

I am sad to have to admit that it took three and a half years for God to overcome my religious prejudices. The first hurdle was recognizing Father Norbert as my brother in Christ. That hurdle was overcome rather quickly. As I got to know Father Norbert, as I witnessed the vitality of his faith and the consistency of his obedient submission to the Spirit and the Scriptures, I was not only convinced of his relationship with the Savior, but challenged in my own walk with Christ. The second hurdle was more difficult to overcome. I was still plagued by the question: How can Father Norbert be an obedient disciple of Jesus Christ and remain a practicing Roman Catholic priest? The words of Paul Billheimer, a former radio pastor and Bible College president, helped me to understand that this is a question between Father Norbert and God, and not a question between Father Norbert and *me:*

> If you are scripturally born again you are a member of the Body of Christ and a son of my very own Father. As a member of the same family, you are my own brother, whether you realize it or acknowledge it or not. As far as I am concerned, this is true whether you are a Charismatic or anti-Charismatic; whether you believe that everyone should speak in tongues or whether you believe that speaking in tongues is of the devil; whether you believe that the gifts of the Spirit are in operation in the Church today or whether you believe they ceased at the close of the Apostolic age; whether you are an Arminian and believe in eternal security or in falling from grace; whether you accept only the "King James" or prefer a modern version; whether you believe in baptismal regeneration or no ordinances at all; whether you believe in immersion or sprinkling, infant or adult baptism; whether you wash feet or don't; whether you are a Methodist, Baptist, Presbyterian, Disciples of Christ, Church of Christ, Mennonite, Amish, Seventh Day Adventist, Episcopalian, Catholic...or no denomination at all; whether you believe in female or only male ordination; whether you think that Saturday is the true Sabbath and should be kept holy or whether you think that the day is indifferent; whether you eat meat or are a vegetarian; whether you drink coffee, tea and soft drinks or only water, fruit juices and milk; whether you wear a toupee or sport a bald head; whether you color your hair or not; whether you are a pre-, a post-, or an amillennialist; whether you are a Republican, a Democrat or a Socialist; whether your skin is white, black, red, brown or yellow; and if there be any other doubtful matters...over which we differ...if you are born again, we are still members of the same family and organic parts of the same spiritual Body. *I may think some of your beliefs are as crazy as a loon, but if I have sufficient love for God, agape love, I will not reject you as a person.*[3]

As I got to know Father Norbert I began to realize that God's family extends beyond the limits of my own church denomination and reaches even into unexpected places. Perhaps Jesus was alluding to this reality when he said: "I have other sheep that are not of this sheep pen. I must bring them also. They too will listen to my voice, and there shall be one flock and one shepherd" (Jn 10:16). I learned through a slow, painful, and drawn-out process that my ability to fellowship with Father Norbert could not be based on shared theological understandings, liturgical practices, or on concepts and opinions concerning "non-essentials." If we were to come together it would have to be on agreement over Evangelical truths which are basic to salvation and on our common life in Christ.

When God broke into my world and showed me that He has sons and daughters in the Roman Catholic Church in France, it was as though He had set off a bomb in my life. Up to that point my church-planting mission in France made sense. As long as I could assume that the church either did not exist in France, or that if it did exist it was so weakened and compromised by its history that it should be replaced, my mission was clear. Now, however, God had brought me to a different appraisal of the situation.

## THE SHIFT FROM CHURCH-*PLANTING* ◆◆ TO CHURCH-*SERVING* ◆◆

This new understanding of the contemporary spiritual scene in France raised a whole new set of questions that needed to be addressed as I reformulated my understanding of my missionary task. For example: Is it really necessary for me to establish a "new church" in France? How seriously should I take the faith and witness of the ancient Church in this land? What would be my most appropriate response, as the cultural "outsider" and "guest" in France, to the spiritual needs of the French? What was I supposed to do with these Christian brothers and sisters? Should I ignore them or just pray for them? What sort of relationship was God leading me to establish with them?

One of the important biblical texts that God impressed on me is found in the seventeenth chapter of John's gospel. I began to wonder if I could effectively witness for Christ in France if I ignored what Francis Schaeffer had called "the final apologetic."[4]

Jesus spoke of it in John 17:21, 23 while He was praying for His disciples. He asked the Father:

> That all of them may be one, Father, just as you are in me and I am in you. May they also be one in us so that the world may believe that you have sent me...I in them and you in me. May they be brought to complete unity to let the world know that you sent me and have loved them even as you have loved me.

According to the prayer of Jesus recorded in this section of Scripture, I felt that I had to be careful not to be divisive in the way in which I ministered.

A second text of Scripture that God used to form my thinking at this juncture is found in Paul's letter to the Philippians. In chapter two, verses three and four we read: "Do nothing out of selfish ambition or vain conceit, but in humility consider others better than yourselves. Each of you should look not only to your own interests, but also to the interests of others." Paul goes on to explain how Jesus Christ put aside His own divine rights and prerogatives so as to bring us salvation.

The teaching of these two texts, coupled with my own missionary experience in the French Catholic world brought me to grapple with some other very important questions: How can I minister in France in such a way that I do not create unnecessary barriers between members of God's household? What are some of the "rights" and "privileges" that God might be calling me as an Evangelical Protestant missionary to abandon, so as to serve Him obediently in France? Recognizing that through my Evangelical Christian heritage God has given me a unique set of skills, understandings and convictions, how can I best use them to serve His work in France? Is it legitimate to attempt to lead French men and women to Christ in a way that reinforces their appreciation of their own Christian heritage? Is it possible to form a community of believers in a locale in which our individual converts find spiritual nourishment and encouragement, without institutionalizing that community—so that the members of that community can remain members of institutional churches and work for renewal within those churches? To what extent is our pursuit of interpersonal unity with individual Catholic believers enhanced or hampered by organizational unity with the Catholic Church (or lack thereof)?

## Stripping Ourselves of All Privilege

As I looked for answers to these questions it became increasingly clear that there were certain rights and privileges that God was calling me to abandon in order to enter into service to the people He already had in France. For example, I had to strip myself of the "right" to be seen as the equal of the clergy of the Roman Catholic Church (which does not recognize the legitimacy of my ordination). I had to rid myself of the "privilege" of preaching the Word of God from the pulpit each Sunday. I was forced to abandon the prerogatives of those who minister in a highly visible, liturgical and sacramental way. I had to give up my right to celebrate the Lord's Supper, to baptize, to marry, to bury. All of these "rights" that I felt were mine because of my own ordination would have to be abandoned if I was to move from a ministry whose aim is to plant independent Evangelical Protestant churches to one which is not divisive and which serves the existing people of God in France.

## Changing Our Ways of Thinking

I recognized that my ways of thinking needed to change. When I arrived in France I operated out of a perspective that asked: "Which group of believers has the most perfect understanding of what it means to be Christ's follower?" This mentality was formed by the Pietist individualism of my faith tradition which clearly taught the obligation to separate from those believers with whom one disagreed over issues of doctrine or practice. Even after I had come to the realization that an individual could be a practicing Roman Catholic and an obedient disciple of Jesus Christ, this mentality continued to plague me. I continued for a long time to feel that the Catholics had everything to learn from me and nothing to teach me. I operated from the perspective that I had arrived at a more perfect understanding of the truth than my Catholic brothers and sisters (otherwise I would have become a Catholic myself).

Slowly, God shifted my thinking so that my preoccupying thought became: "How can I bring the light which I have received from my own faith tradition and religious heritage and serve the followers of Christ in this place?" I began to understand that I had things to learn from, as well as contribute to, the faith of my Catholic brothers and sisters. Not one of us has arrived at a complete understanding of God's self-revelation. No single faith community has appropriated all of God's truth. We are all pilgrims. We are all in process. And we need each other.

The apostle Paul reminds us that in Jesus of Nazareth the divine took the form of a servant. Servants exist to serve and to meet needs. When God broke into my world in 1979 and revealed to me that He has a people in the Catholic Church, one of my first reactions was, "Then why did You lead me here? What are the needs experienced by Your people in this place that You want to meet through the unique equipping and preparation that You have given to me via my own spiritual heritage?" As I have meditated on these questions, several broad areas of spiritual need of the French have come to my attention. I will not take the time to develop these here, but if you are interested in reading more on this subject, I refer you to my book *Unfamiliar Paths: The Challenge of Recognizing the Work of Christ in Strange Clothing.*[5]

## ◆◆  UNFAMILIAR PATHS  ◆◆

In Isaiah 42:16 we read God's words to His servant:

> I will lead the blind by ways they have not known,
>     along unfamiliar paths I will guide them;
> I will turn the darkness into light before them
>     and make the rough places smooth.
> These are the things I will do;
>     I will not forsake them.

How difficult it is for us to walk along unfamiliar paths! The inner struggles of such an experience become even more apparent when we add the fact that we are blind to where these paths might be leading us.

When we began our missionary work in France in 1979, we did not imagine that it would look like it does today. We thought that it would be similar to what we had already experienced. We assumed that God would lead us along a more familiar trail. Instead, God has led us into situations where we have felt very uncomfortable. He has forced us to open our eyes to realities that we did not want to face. He has taught us that even if, after eighteen years of ministry in France, we don't have definitive answers to give to the questions listed above, that's okay. Sometimes in our desire to arrive at our destination we forget that in God's view the trip is at least as important as the arrival. In other words, God seems to be just as interested in our walk of faith as He is in our arriving at the "right" understandings.

Diane and I were not alone in our ministry pilgrimage. The leaders of the mission who had sent us to France also found themselves on unfamiliar turf as a result of the direction that our ministry was taking. In 1982 the Overseas Director of our mission wrote me a letter asking: "What are you guys doing in France? Are you going to start a Missionary Church or not?" This was a very logical question. Wherever the Missionary Church had sent missionaries in the past they had planted Missionary Church churches, and Diane and I had been sent to France with the expectation that we would do likewise. My response to his inquiry probably did little to quiet his fears:

> We find ourselves confronted with the dilemma facing every Protestant missionary working in France. Are we going to insist on identity with the Missionary Church for these converts, and thus become ineffective in evangelism and divisive of the Body of Christ? Or are we institutionally humble enough to put God's purposes above our own? Will we continue to allow these French men and women to come to Christ through the small Bible discussion groups? Or will we

begin erecting unnecessary barriers by insisting that they identify with the Missionary Church?

A few years later our church denomination joined a Protestant Evangelical association that had taken a strong stand against Roman Catholicism. When we had been in France almost ten years, they wrote to us saying: "Wait a minute. We are members of this association of Evangelicals. Is what you are doing in France in line with this association's stance toward the Roman Catholic faith?" At that point I wrote a 130-page paper in which I analyzed our ministry from three perspectives: a biblical perspective, a historical perspective, and a cultural perspective. In that paper I showed that from all three of these perspectives, what we were doing was legitimate.

I am not sure that the members of the missions board actually read that paper, but they called me home from the field and met with me behind locked doors on three occasions. The last of these meetings took several hours. During the discussions there was tremendous opposition to our approach to the ministry in France. After lengthy, animated talks the board was ready to take a vote on whether or not to close down their work in France, yank my credentials, and so forth. I was spent emotionally, so I left the room and went out into the hallway to wait for their decision.

They took their vote, after which a man came and joined me in the hall. This man had been a missionary in Africa for about twenty-five years. He said, "You know, Dave, I've never in all my experience seen such a powerful demonstration of God's ability to change human hearts as what took place right before that vote was taken." He told me that the one man who had been the most vocal in his opposition to what was happening in our ministry in France stood up and said, "I don't like what they're doing in France. I think it's wrong, but somehow I sense God is in it, and I won't vote against the Spirit of God!" So the vote was unanimous that we be allowed to continue.

People who know the Missionary Church denomination scratch their heads in amazement and say, "How in the world could they let you do what you are doing?"

*Evangelical Protestant Responses to Our Ministry*

There is often opposition when God leads us along unfamiliar paths! I have been banned from the pulpits of some Missionary Churches. I have received ugly, nasty letters—from pastors! I have even had letters circulated against me by ex-Catholics who feel that I should be cut off from all fellowship with Evangelical Protestant believers.

On the other hand many Evangelical Protestant laypeople seem to understand and accept more easily than their clergy the new ways in which God has led us to minister in France. I have often been surprised and overwhelmed by the positive response of North American laypeople to our ministry. They seem to grasp the concepts and weigh the risks very quickly. On numerous occasions, with tears in their eyes, they have said things like: "Some of my best friends are Roman Catholics. I know how deeply they love our Lord. It hurts me to hear some of the things that our pastor says about Catholics." On one occasion an elderly fellow shared how it was his Catholic friend who led him to faith in Christ, although he had grown up in a Baptist environment. Others express their disgust over the numerous divisions within the Christian family of faith. There have been some cases where individuals have mentioned the hurt that they felt because, coming from a Roman Catholic background and now belonging to an Evangelical Protestant church, they felt isolated and misunderstood by their own parents, brothers and sisters, or other family members. Our ministry in France seemed to give these people the assurance that some of those barriers could be overcome. Alongside the pastors and theologians in the Evangelical Protestant world who feel that we have betrayed the Reformation and "gone off the deep end," we must place these positive testimonies of comprehension and acceptance.

Among the members of the missionary community we find the same mixed reaction to our ministry. Some find it full of discernment and hope, while others have serious reservations concerning our approach. Some commend us for plowing new ground, while others feel that we have failed to call people out of their Catholic culture in an appropriate manner.

## Roman Catholic Responses to Our Ministry

When we were led along the unfamiliar path of ministry in service to the Catholic Church in France, there were a number of very practical questions that needed to be addressed. Where would we attend church services? What kind of religious education would we give to our own children? If we refused to perform the sacraments ourselves, in what context could we and our children, or our converts, experience this vital aspect of the Christian experience?

It seemed natural that if we were called to serve Roman Catholic believers, then we should worship where they worship. This we decided to do. We began by having our parish priests over for dinner in order to get acquainted with them, and to let them know how God had been leading our lives and ministry. We informed them of our Evangelical Protestant identity and assured them that we were willing to serve them in any way they felt appropriate. We expressed our desire to be as discreet as possible at Mass so as not to offend any of the members of the parish. At the same time, I began auditing courses at the local Catholic seminary on the meaning of the liturgy, the Catholic understanding of the Eucharist, and so on. I wanted to understand, as much as possible, the meaning of the Catholic Mass from the Catholic perspective.

Our children attended catechism classes in our local parish, and when they had made a personal commitment of their lives to Christ, each of them chose to be baptized by our parish priest.

I also contacted our local Catholic bishop and asked for a meeting, which he graciously agreed to. This was the first of several meetings that I would have with our bishop through the years. During that meeting I once again explained our Evangelical Protestant origins as well as the unique way in which God seemed to be leading us in service to Catholics in France. The reception that we received from the bishop was at times warm and accepting, and at other times cold and judgmental. Sometimes he would

affirm that "no one else can do the work of evangelism in the
parish that you are doing," or that wherever we were involved the
"church is strengthened." But at other times he would express his
feeling that we might be some kind of religious "spies" who "infil-
trate" the Catholic Church with the hope of drawing people away
from the church of their origin.

Our approach to ministry in France brought us to encounter
the resistance of Catholic clergy and lay leaders who felt that we
should not be trusted. Some of these people had had bad experiences with Evangelical Protestants in the past; others, for political
reasons, did not want to reach out in a way that other Catholic
leaders might not understand or appreciate.

On the positive side, some Catholic leaders opened their arms
and hearts to us and recognized that we could assist them in some of
their areas of need. This was the case for the director of one Catholic
Middle school in our town who, along with the school chaplain,
invited me to teach catechism classes. For six years I taught catechism classes in that school. I was also asked to help prepare young
people for Confirmation and for a couple of years served on the Pastoral Committee of the school. Diane, too, found an open reception
in our parish where she helped with catechism classes.

On the negative side were the Catholic leaders who believed
that "Catholics and Evangelicals are like oil and water—they don't
mix!" Some of these individuals felt that we were too biblical in our
approach and that our converts displayed too many Evangelical
Protestant traits. Others felt that our converts took their faith too
seriously and had become "more Catholic than the pope." While
these detractors could not deny that nonbelievers were coming to
Christ and reintegrating the Church through our ministry, they
didn't like the idea of having an Evangelical pastor in their midst.

◆◆     CONCLUSION     ◆◆

Andrew Walls, one of the leading historians of Christian missions, has written: "Europe has become a prime area, perhaps *the*
prime area, for identification as a mission field."[6] His view is

based on the observation that a majority of present-day Europeans can be described as "ignorant of religion," "immoral," "prone to warfare," "inhumane," and "widely accepting of injustice." These words, which were formerly used to characterize peoples living outside of the territories of historical Christendom, now apply to Europeans who demonstrate marked recession from Christian commitment. The importance of reaching these modern "heathens" is driven home by the stirring call of Karl Rahner in *The Shape of the Church to Come:*

> The possibility...of winning new Christians from a milieu that has become unchristian is the sole living and convincing evidence that even today Christianity still has a real chance for the future.[7]

Our ministry in France has led us to believe that this post-Christendom area of the world will not be significantly influenced for Christ in our day unless we learn to recognize the new and varied ways in which He is presently at work! Nor will we witness an important turning to God on the part of the French until we experience a more perfect unity with other followers of Jesus of Nazareth (Jn 17:21). Evangelical Protestant missionaries will not win significant numbers of new Christians from unchristian France by working in isolation from or in opposition to their Roman Catholic brothers and sisters. Nor will Roman Catholics win significant numbers of new Christians from unchristian France by working in isolation from or in opposition to their Evangelical Protestant brothers and sisters.

## Notes

1. Pierce R. Beaver, *To Advance the Gospel: Selections From the Writings of Rufus Anderson* (Grand Rapids, Mich.: Eerdmans, 1967), 107.

2. Donald M. McGavran, *How Churches Grow* (New York: Friendship Press, 1973), 17.

3. Paul Billheimer, *Love Covers* (Fort Washington, Pa.: Christian Literature Crusade, 1981), 114 (emphasis added).

4. Francis A. Schaeffer, *The Church at the End of the Twentieth Century* (Downers Grove: InterVarsity, 1970), 138.

5. (Pasadena, Calif.: William Carey, 1997).

6. Andrew F. Walls, *The Missionary Movement in Christian History* (New York: Orbis, 1996), 258.

7. Karl Rahner, *The Shape of the Church to Come* (New York: Seabury, 1974), 32.

# Afterword

*Edward Idris Cardinal Cassidy*

From a reading of the various articles that make up the present book, it is obvious that something of great significance has been taking place in recent years with respect to relations between two of the largest Christian world communions, Evangelicals and Catholics.

These two Christian communities remain far apart in respect of their doctrinal understanding of the Gospel and its teaching. Yet at the same time they often find themselves sharing a common approach to ethical questions and to other matters relating to the public forum.

Even with regard to fundamental elements of Christian faith, there has been in recent years a new realization that Evangelicals and Catholics are not so far distant one from the other as had been taken for granted. Much of the past polemics and dissent resulted from misconceptions, stereotypes and myths concerning the other's teaching. A deeper understanding of the teaching of the other has resulted from members of the two communities coming together in a frank exchange on fundamental Christian beliefs.

An outstanding contribution to this process has been made by Rev. Richard Neuhaus and Charles Colson. Their publication *Evangelicals and Catholics Together* has shown that there is much that members of these two communities can say together, while pointing out at the same time the questions on which they remain divided. Although this work was not the result of an official dialogue and has not been universally received by the communities concerned, it remains a valuable contribution to better understanding between the two expressions of Christian understanding and has already contributed significantly to better Catholic-Evangelical relations.

I was fortunate to be part of an informal meeting that followed on the publication of *Evangelicals and Catholics Together,* held in New York in September 1997. Several members of CELAM took part and a precious and fruitful exchange of views led to the publication of a paper by Timothy George on "The Gift of Salvation."[1]

In this study, as later in the historic *Joint Declaration on the Doctrine of Justification* signed in Augsburg, Germany, on October 31, 1999, between the Catholic Church and the Lutheran World Federation, it is shown that on basic truths of the fundamental question of salvation or justification there is common agreement between Catholics and many Evangelicals. For over 400 years misunderstandings concerning the Catholic doctrine on Justification have been at the heart of much of the aggressive attitude toward the "evangelization" of Catholics by other Christian communities.

Particularly encouraging for the work of Christian Unity are recent developments that have taken place in this regard in Latin America. Already in New York we heard of several experiences of cooperation in various fields of Christian activity and pastoral care bringing together Evangelical and Catholic pastors, as for example in the prison apostolate. Then in May 1998 a meeting took place in Quito, Ecuador, organized jointly by CELAM and CLAI, with the participation of evangelical leaders from different countries of Latin America. The declaration produced at these meetings sets out certain basic principles that, if accepted and put into practice, could change radically the relationship of Evangelicals and Catholics in Latin American countries.[2]

I would wish also to draw attention to the official dialogues that are taking place under the auspices of the Pontifical Council for Promoting Christian Unity. I refer in the first place to the theological consultations jointly sponsored by the Pontifical Council and the World Evangelical Fellowship's Theological Commission. The third such consultation was held from November 7 to November 13, 1999, in Wisconsin, USA. The final *Comuniqué* stated: "As we listened jointly to the Scriptures, prayed together, and spoke the truth to one another in love, we recognized and rejoiced in the fellowship we have in Christ based on our common faith in Him. The riches of this gift are such that all who share in it cannot regard each other as strangers much less treat each other as enemies." The consultation achieved "considerable agreement about the Christian responsibility to promote in public life the rights of individuals and communities to religious freedom," and affirmed that "Christians can collaborate together in love and mutual respect even though their fellowship is incomplete." Moreover, it was agreed that these theological conversations will now go forward on a regular basis.

A second promising dialogue is the Pentecostal/Roman Catholic International Dialogue that has been organized for a number of years by the Pontifical Council for Promoting Christian Unity and some Classical Pentecostal leaders. Again, we have proof that such a dialogue is possible and can produce good results when Christians of even such diverse traditions come together in sincere and frank encounter. This dialogue has recently produced an excellent common statement on the difficult question of *Evangelization, Proselytism and Common Witness* that deserves wide attention within the ecumenical movement.[3]

Mention should also be made of the Southern Baptist/Roman Catholic Conversation, sponsored over the past thirty years by the Secretariat for Ecumenical and Interreligious Affairs of the United States National Conference of Catholic Bishops. In September of this year, the Conversation published a report of the discussions of the past five years on Sacred Scripture. The participants declare: "We have met as both Roman Catholic and Southern Baptist institutions, and at each gathering we have shared together in the reading of Scripture and in common prayer. In the context of patient listening and candid sharing with one another, we have each read and reported on documents in the two traditions that illustrate our points of agreement and disagreement." They conclude the report with the affirmation that "we have learned a great deal from each other. We will continue this conversation on other themes that concern our Christian faith."

Very recently I attended a conference in Moscow on the theme: Jesus Christ, the Same Yesterday, Today and Forever—Christianity at the Threshold of the Third Millennium. This brought together Russian Orthodox, Catholics, and Protestants. Certainly, there is much tension in Russia and the CIS over the activities of certain Evangelical Christians and sects. Despite this, the November 1999 Conference in Moscow was a sign that even in such a situation, Orthodox, Catholic and Evangelical Christians can come together fruitfully.

I leave the reader with a personal reflection on these developments. Catholics and Evangelicals have in common their fundamental belief in Jesus Christ as their Savior. They share a similar vision on many questions concerning life and morals. As they cross together the threshold of a new Christian Millennium, Catholics and Evangelicals will be challenged with many identical problems. Their primary concern will be how to defend and promote fundamental Christian values in an ever more pluralistic, secularized society deeply influenced by neo-liberalism and unbridled consumerism. Surely this challenge should urge these two communities to rid themselves of all misunderstandings, stereotypes and myths about the other and encourage them to join their powerful forces in a common struggle to conserve their Christian heritage and its fundamental values. This seems to me to be a service to the world of the twenty-first century, to which they are called by the Lord himself.

## Notes

1. Timothy George, "Evangelicals and Catholics Together: A New Initiative" *Christianity Today* (December 8, 1997), 34–38.

2. Encuentro Católico-Pentecostal Latinoamericano y Caribeño, *Mensaje a las Iglesias*, Quito (Ecuador), Mayo 12–14 de 1998, in: *Medellin 95*, Vol. XXIV, 524–527.

3. Pentecostal/Roman Catholic International Dialogue, "Evangelisation, Proselytism and Common Witness," *Information Service*, 97/I–II (1998), 38–56.

# Contributors

*David E. Bjork,* a pastor in the Missionary Church, is a Ph.D. candidate in theology at the Institut Catholique of Paris and in religious science at the Sorbonne. For the past twenty years he has been doing missionary work in France, working with Roman Catholic communities in the area of evangelism, discipleship, and leadership training for their parishioners. He lives with his wife in Dijon.

*Gerald Bray* is a priest of the Church of England and currently Anglican Professor of Divinity at Beeson Divinity School, Samford University, Birmingham, Alabama. He has written a number of books on different theological subjects, and has recently edited the post-Reformation Anglican canons.

*Edward Idris Cardinal Cassidy* is the President of the Pontifical Council for Promoting Christian Unity in Rome.

*Avery Dulles, S.J.*, is the Lawrence J. McGinley Professor of Religion and Society at Fordham University, Bronx, New York. The author of nineteen major books and over six hundred articles, he is a past president of the Catholic Theological Society of America and served on the International Theological Commission in Rome.

*Timothy George* is the founding dean of Beeson Divinity School, Samford University, and senior adviser at *Christianity Today.* He is a member of the Southern Baptist-Roman Catholic Conversation Team and has participated in the Evangelicals and Catholics Together initiative.

*Richard J. Mouw* is President of Fuller Theological Seminary in Pasadena, California. Before coming to Fuller in 1985 as professor of Christian philosophy and ethics, he was for seventeen years professor of philosophy at Calvin College in Grand Rapids, Michigan.

*Thomas P. Rausch, S.J.*, is the T. Marie Chilton Professor of Catholic Theology and chair of the Department of Theological Studies at Loyola Marymount University in Los Angeles. A specialist in the areas of ecclesiology and ecumenism, he is a member of the Catholic/Southern Baptist Conversation and co-chairs the Los Angeles Catholic/Evangelical Committee.

*Cecil M. Robeck, Jr.*, Associate Professor of Church History and Ecumenics at Fuller Theological Seminary, Pasadena, is an Assemblies of God minister. He belongs to both the WCC and NCC Faith and Order Commissions, co-chairs the Pentecostal/Roman Catholic and Pentecostal/World Alliances of Reformed Churches dialogues and the Los Angeles Catholic/Evangelical Committee. He also represents the worldwide Pentecostal movement with the Secretaries of Christian World Communions.

*Robert Louis Wilken,* a historian of Christian thought, is the William R. Kenan, Jr., Professor of the History of Christianity at the University of Virginia. His most recent book is *Remembering the*

*Christian Past* (Wm. B. Eerdmans, 1995). He is a former president of the American Academy of Religion and an elected fellow of the American Academy of Arts and Sciences.